ANOTHER WEEK IN

The Kitchen

ANOTHER WEEK IN
The Kitchen

KAREN DUDLEY

with Russel Wasserfall & Roxanne Spears

a few words

The Kitchen opened its doors in April 2009 without much fanfare. While we were cleaning and fixing and fitting out our tiny shop, passers-by knocked on the doors asking when we were planning to open. They were hungry. But our projections were conservative, bleak even. Who would come? Woodstock was the place you had your car audio fitted, or you bought some fabric. But eating?

Our first customers were a couple from a gallery in the neighbourhood. She was sad, a little teary. He was attentive, kind. This was not the moment for me to show off and impress with all our fare. I knew what I had to do: administer a pot of tea and a Lemon Square.

And here was my epiphany: I love to serve! I could touch people with food. This was my *thing*: to make something simple and delicious *to reach to the heart!* I could listen, watch, and then offer food to console, comfort, intrigue or inspire.

In *A Week in The Kitchen* I offered my recipes and received the greatest joy I could wish for: people embracing these flavours and making them their own. People who had never cooked before were now cooking their way through the book, cover to cover! Other readers were cooking their way out of grief. People were buying books for children, sisters or brothers, aunts, uncles and mothers. My act of devotion was being received and shared many times over!

Another Week in The Kitchen reveals some of the jewels that have been set amongst the old, favourite recipes. You will find many recipes to add to your repertoire with familiar confidence, but there are also new flavours to stretch your skills and imagination. May these recipes bring pleasure in the sharing.

contents

Monday

Phati's Spring Green Salad with Sumac

This salad is so very beautiful. It plays with my favourite colour combination, green and pink. The blanched green medley (you could add fresh broad beans, mange-touts or fine beans) is sweet and delicious with the creamy feta and the zingy dressing.

1 packet of sugar snap peas, trimmed
    and stringed
2 cups frozen baby peas (petit pois)
Sea salt
1 bunch radishes, trimmed and
    thinly sliced
100g Danish feta
2 tbsp coarsely chopped fresh mint
Rainbow peppercorns, freshly ground

Dressing
3 tbsp extra-virgin olive oil
1 tbsp fresh lemon juice
1 tbsp Dijon mustard
1 tsp white wine vinegar
½ tsp sumac * + more for garnish

Blanch the sugar snaps in boiling water for no longer than 2–3 minutes. Strain with a large slotted spoon into a colander and rinse thoroughly with cold water or transfer to a bowl of ice water to arrest the cooking process. Slice the sugar snap peas in half across the middle to reveal the delicate peas inside. Blanch the peas in the boiling water from the sugar snaps. Once the peas have surfaced (usually 2–3 minutes), drain in a colander, rinse with cold water or immerse in an icy bath. Drain and set aside.

To make the dressing, whisk the oil, lemon juice, Dijon mustard, vinegar and sumac in a small bowl.

To assemble the salad, layer the peas, sliced sugar snaps and radishes on a platter. Drizzle over the sumac vinaigrette. Garnish with crumbled feta, chopped mint, the ground rainbow peppercorns and the remaining sumac. Once dressed, eat immediately.

Serves 8

* You can find the sour sumac spice in speciality delis

Parmesan Cauliflower

I shamelessly make food to reach straight to the heart. This Parmesan Cauliflower makes it so easy!

3 heads of cauliflower, cut into florets
4 eggs, lightly beaten
2½ cup panko breadcrumbs
3 cups vegetable oil, for frying
1 cup grated Parmesan
2 tbsp ching ching (see page 221)

Combine the breadcrumbs, Parmesan and ching ching in a bowl. Toss 5–6 florets at a time into the bowl of beaten egg, then toss the egg-coated florets into the Parmesan-seasoned breadcrumbs to coat. Fry the crumbed cauliflower in batches for about 5–6 minutes over medium heat until golden brown. Remove with a slotted spoon to a tray or plate covered with paper towel to drain. Serve as soon as possible. Your friends will gobble these up!

Serves 8

Red Rice with Cranberries

I was in Nebraska when I first tasted fresh cranberries. My taste buds screamed, "Now this is sour!" So, yes, it is sugar that transforms them, but it is the hint of sourness that makes cranberries the perfect partner, in flavour and colour, to the red rice.

250g red rice (or basmati or black rice)
2 cups cranberries (or sour cherries if
    you're lucky enough to get your hands
    on them)
10 spring onions, cleaned and sliced
5 radishes, finely sliced
1 cup of flaked almonds, toasted
30g Italian parsley, chopped

Dressing
2 juniper berries, crushed
½ tsp thyme
2 tsp sour cherry jam or cranberry jelly
4 tsp vinegar
Zest and juice of 1 orange
5 tbsp olive oil or half-half with hazelnut
    or walnut oil
Salt and course ground black pepper

Boil the red rice in plenty of water for about 30 minutes, then drain in a colander and rinse with cold water.

Place the cooled rice, cranberries, spring onions, radishes and most of the flaked almonds in a large bowl and season with salt and black pepper.

Whisk all the dressing ingredients together in a small bowl and pour over the salad.

Toss in the parsley at the very last moment so as not to lose any of its greenness in this red, red salad.

Serves 8

Smacked Cucumber in Chinese Sauce

This is the only recipe in this book advocating a mild form of violence. Food made with calm and care can only be good, but in this case, the smacking breaks the cucumber's integrity so that, broken, it takes on this sublime Chinese dressing.

4 cucumbers
1½ tsp salt

Sauce
1 tbsp finely chopped garlic
3 tbsp caster sugar
½ cup light soya sauce
½ cup Chinese black vinegar
1 tbsp chilli oil
1 tsp Chinese 5 Spice

Lay the cucumber on a chopping board and smack it hard a few times with the flat blade of a Chinese cleaver or with a rolling pin. Partially peel the cucumber, then cut it, lengthways, into four pieces. Hold your knife at an angle to the chopping board and cut the cucumber on the diagonal into ½ cm slices. Place in a bowl with the salt and mix well and set aside for about 10 minutes.

Combine all the other ingredients in a small bowl. Drain the cucumber, pour over the sauce, stir well and serve.

Serves 8

Sumac-Roasted Tomatoes with Currants & White Beans

With such a wealth of amazing restaurants in Istanbul, we just knew that they weren't buying their spices from the spice market. So with eyes bright and vigilant, my sweetheart and I set off in search of where Stramboulis bought their spices. Unmoved by the piles of open spices set out for tourists, we went through the market, past the white cheese vendors, and turned left at a large square just before the docks of the Bosphorus. And there – like the grail – were deep, wooden boxes of the best spices. And the kind shopkeeper-guide showed me the sumac ground and unground. The finest cumin. Dried sour cherries. And much more. My husband was very patient. He knew I needed to take some time. You can find the sour oxblood-coloured sumac spice in speciality delis. We sell it at The Kitchen too.

16 plum tomatoes, halved
   (or 800g cherry tomatoes)
2 tsp sumac
8 garlic cloves, thinly sliced
1 red onion, finely chopped
30g sweet basil, leaves only,
   larger leaves torn
6 tsp brown sugar
½ tsp ground cinnamon
Salt
100 ml olive oil
100g currants, soaked in 1 cup hot
water for 20 minutes and drained
2 tins cannellini beans, drained
Black pepper
20g fresh basil leaves or roughly
   chopped Italian parsley

Preheat the oven to 200°C.

Place the tomatoes in a shallow roasting dish. Combine the sumac, garlic, red onion, basil, sugar and cinnamon in a small bowl and season with salt. Scatter this mixture over the tomatoes and drizzle olive oil over the top. Roast for 5 minutes and then turn the oven off and leave overnight without opening the oven at all. If you need your tomatoes sooner, turn the oven down to 140°C and roast for 50 minutes.

Remove the roasting tray from the oven, scatter the currants over the top and then roast at 190°C for a further 15 minutes until the tomatoes are soft and caramelised.

Place the drained cannellini beans on a serving platter and season with salt and black pepper and a splash of olive oil. Gently toss the tomato mixture through the beans with all the juices of the pan (a great dressing). Garnish with basil leaves or the roughly chopped parsley.

Serves 8

Minute Maid Slaw

My daughter, Maggie, is named after my kind and wise great-aunt Maggie who lived in Castletown Road, Wittebome. My brother and I have fond memories of staying with her. A retired teacher, we remember her twittering aviary, sweetpeas growing in abundance up strings in her back yard, and the wondrous ice-cold Minute Maid she would give us in the afternoons when we came back from school. Here is a dressing capitalising on the intensity of this orange concentrate.

⅓ cup frozen orange juice
    concentrate, thawed
⅓ cup rice vinegar
⅓ cup vegetable oil
Salt and pepper
1 medium white cabbage or about
    4 cups cabbage, finely sliced
4 mealies, boiled for 6 minutes,
    kernels cut from the cob
2 medium carrots, peeled and
    coarsely grated
1 red pepper, stemmed and cut
    into thin strips
6 spring onions, thinly sliced
½ cup chopped fresh coriander

Whisk the orange juice concentrate, rice vinegar and vegetable oil in a small bowl. Season with salt and pepper and set aside. Combine the finely sliced cabbage, corn kernels, carrots, red pepper, spring onion and coriander in a large bowl. Toss with enough dressing to coat. Season the slaw with salt and pepper to taste. Allow to stand for a while for the dressing and vegetables to become acquainted. Toss again and serve.

Serves 8

Baby Spinach with Gomashio & Flaxseed Oil

My very dear friend Rhian Berning and her family have chosen a life of conscious living surrounded by indigenous forests, mountains and fynbos on a hill in beautiful Plettenberg Bay. On one memorable weekend away, she introduced me to this marriage of baby spinach, flaxseed oil and flaked sea salt. You can only imagine how ridiculously good it is for you!

700g baby spinach
3–4 tbsp flaxseed oil
1–2 tsp gomashio (see page 220)
2 avocados, sliced into wedges (optional)
2 oranges, completely peeled, membranes
    removed to free segments (optional)

Toss the spinach and the flaxseed oil in a large salad bowl to lightly coat the leaves. If using, add the avo and orange segments. Sprinkle with the gomashio. Serve immediately.

Serves 8

Our Own Corned Beef

I couldn't have been more proud. We removed our first corned (salted) beef from its poaching pot and cut into the fall-apart pink flesh. We were all oohs and aahs. Here was a triumph! Our own corned beef: a truly nostalgic way of presenting a cheaper and relatively neglected cut of meat. And so, so much nicer than shop-bought corned beef.

5 kg beef brisket, deboned
   (about 2 2.5 kg slabs)
2 carrots
2 onions
1 celery stick
1 leek
Selection of French herbs
½ head of garlic

Brine
550g light brown sugar
700g coarse salt
4 tsp black peppercorns
1 tbsp juniper berries (or 5 star aniseed)
10 cloves
8 bay leaves
Small bunch of thyme, crushed
110g saltpetre

Put all the brine ingredients into a large pot, pour in 5 l of water and gradually bring to a boil, stirring to help the sugar and salt dissolve. Once it comes to a boil, let it bubble away for 2 minutes. Take off the heat and allow to cool completely.

Pierce the meat all over with a skewer. Place in a large, sterilised plastic box and cover the meat with the brine. It must be completely immersed. Refrigerate for 7 days. Check every few days or so that the meat is entirely immersed and turning a beautiful pink.

We weight down the meat with a full bottle of wine or vinegar so that the meat gets a full baptism.

After a week, take the meat out of the brine, rinse, and then roll and tie the beef to secure it while boiling. Put the beef together with the carrots, onions, celery, leek, any French herbs you may have and the garlic. Bring the water to the boil and then simmer very gently on the stove top for 2–3 hours. Cook until the meat is completely tender.

Serve warm or cold with horseradish or mustard, pickles or piccalilli, or even a beetroot salad or slaw. The beef will keep, well wrapped, in the fridge for a week. Try it in sandwiches, hash and even added to a slaw.

Serves 8

* Saltpetre can be found at some chemists. You can certainly do the recipe without it but the saltpetre is what gives the corned beef its pink finish.

Green Harissa, Bulgar Wheat with Avo & Peas

Although you could make this salad with couscous, we much prefer it with coarse bulgar wheat. We like how the texture works with the avo and the peas, and how it projects the flavour of this excellent harissa. And any remaining Green Harissa can be frozen and used again at another stage.

Green Harissa
(makes 1½ cups)
1 tbsp cumin seeds
½ tbsp coriander seeds
1½ green chillies, seeded
   and sliced (optional)
2 spring onions, sliced
½ tsp crushed garlic
¼ cup flat-leaf parsley
¼ cup coriander leaves and stems
⅛ cup lemon juice
½ cup extra-virgin olive oil
½ tsp fine sea salt

Salad
1½ cups bulgar wheat
1 cup blanched peas
Salt and pepper
4 spring onions, sliced finely
   on the diagonal
2 avocados, peeled and cut into chunks
1 large handful baby spinach

To make the harissa, lightly toast the cumin and coriander seeds in a small pan over medium heat, stirring often until fragrant, about 2–3 minutes. Allow to cool.

In a food processor, purée the seeds with chillies, spring onions, garlic, parsley, coriander and lemon juice. With the motor running, slowly drizzle in the oil and finally the salt until you have a smooth paste. To store, press a piece of plastic wrap directly onto the surface of the harissa. Cover and chill.

For the salad, bring a deep pot of water to the boil and boil the bulgar wheat for 9–11 minutes. Drain carefully in a small-holed colander or sieve, and rinse with cold water to arrest the cooling process.

Blanch the peas in boiling water for 1 minute. Rinse with cold water and set aside.

To assemble the salad, stir one cup of your green harissa paste through the bulgar wheat and season with salt and black pepper. Gently toss the peas, spring onions, avo and baby spinach through the bulgar, reserving a little of each ingredient to garnish the top of the salad. Arrange the green pile on a beautiful platter. If you like, you could thin the remaining harissa down with ¼ cup more olive oil and drizzle a little over the top of the salad.

Serves 8

Bloody Mary Salad

I love drinking Bloody Marys from those little plastic glasses on aeroplanes. I enjoy them so much, I always swear that I will start making them when I'm back on earth – except, of course, I'll make them in a beautiful glass complete with celery stick. I once saw a picture of this salad spooned over seared steaks and I loved the notion of a tomato salad with Bloody Mary bits (minus the vodka). Although, come to think of it, there's no real reason you shouldn't try it with the vodka!

1½ red onions, finely chopped
1 tbsp sherry vinegar
800g cherry tomatoes or assorted
    beautiful tomatoes, halved
5 celery stalks and leaves, stalks chopped,
    leaves picked + leaves for garnish
½ cup chopped green olives

Dressing
2 tbsp sherry vinegar
2 tbsp prepared horseradish
1½ tbsp Worcestershire sauce
1 tsp Tabasco
½ tsp celery salt
¼ cup olive oil
Sea salt and freshly ground
    black pepper

Mix the onion and 1 tbsp of the sherry vinegar in a large bowl. Allow to macerate for 10 minutes, tossing often. Then add the tomatoes, celery, and olives.

To make the dressing, whisk the remaining sherry vinegar, horseradish, Worcestershire sauce, Tabasco and celery salt in a deeper mixing bowl. Slowly whisk in the olive oil to make a lively vinaigrette. Add the dressing to the tomatoes and other ingredients and toss to coat. Season with salt and black pepper and garnish with the celery leaves. This salad is superb spooned over grilled steaks.

Serves 8

Black Rice Salad with Smoked Salmon, Avo & Dill

This is a rather smart sushi-style salad. You could also serve it, sans smoked salmon, alongside a slow-roasted or grilled salmon trout.

3 cups black rice

4 tbsp rice vinegar

3 tbsp caster sugar

1 tsp salt

6 spring onions, finely sliced
  on the diagonal

½ cup pickled ginger, roughly chopped

1 cup soya bean sprouts

1 Romaine lettuce, leaves finely
  shredded (optional)

160g smoked salmon or salmon trout,
  cut into ½-cm strips

20g dill, sprigs picked

2 avocados, peeled and cut into slices

1 tbsp Japanese rice sprinkle
  or gomashio (see page 220)
  or toasted sesame seeds

Dressing

40g fresh dill

1 egg

1 tbsp English mustard

4 tbsp vinegar

2 tbsp water

2 tbsp caster sugar

¾ cup vegetable oil

Salt and white pepper

To make the dill dressing, put the dill, egg, mustard, vinegar, water and caster sugar in a food processor or the jug of a handheld blender and process to combine. With the motor running, slowly drizzle in the oil to form a rich, creamy dill dressing. Taste and season with salt and white pepper. You might add more mustard at this point or a teaspoon more sugar to taste.

Boil the black rice in plenty of water until tender, about 40 minutes. Watch during cooking that it does not catch and burn.

You might need to add more water. When tender, drain and rinse with cold water.

While the rice is boiling, put the rice vinegar, sugar and salt in a small saucepan and dissolve the sugar and salt over low heat. Allow to cool and season the rice with this mixture. Set aside.

Once you have all the salad ingredients ready, begin by tossing the spring onions, pickled ginger, bean sprouts, shredded lettuce, smoked salmon and dill sprigs gently through the rice with your fingers. You do not want to over mix, just gently distribute the bits through the rice.

Arrange on a beautiful platter, creating little craters in which to nestle the avocado slices. Drizzle a few tablespoons of the dill dressing over the whole salad. Sprinkle with Japanese rice sprinkle, gomashio or toasted sesame seeds.

Serves 8

Potatoes Tartar

This is a great potato salad recipe to have in your arsenal. It has lots of bits in it, which is just what we South Africans love! Just thinking of a still-warm tartared potato makes me weak!

2 kg salad potatoes
4 tbsp capers
3 tbsp chopped gherkins
30g chives, finely snipped
30g flat-leaf parsley, finely chopped
30g dill, finely chopped
6 hard-boiled eggs (7 minutes)
Sea salt and freshly ground black pepper

Dressing
3 tbsp cider vinegar
4 tbsp Dijon mustard
¼ cup olive oil
salt and pepper

Boil the potatoes, whole, in plenty of water. Lower the heat and allow them to simmer for 12–14 minutes until tender.

To make the vinaigrette, put the cider vinegar, mustard, oil and some salt and pepper in a screw-topped jar and shake to emulsify. Drain the potatoes and place in a large bowl. Use your fingers to gently break them into bite-sized pieces. While they are still warm, pour on the vinaigrette and toss to mix. They will become tartar-ed! Leave to cool.

Add the finely chopped capers, gherkins, herbs and more salt and pepper and toss again with your fingers. Arrange on a platter. Quarter the boiled eggs lengthways, and place on top of the salad, moving potatoes here and tucking some eggs into the salad so that everyone gets some.

Serves 8

Beetroot, Fennel & Fig

I love the sweet "meaty" bite of the dried figs in this salad, and how the fragrant fennel connects with the beetroot.

1 kg beetroot
120g sliced dried figs
30g dill, roughly chopped
30g coriander, roughly chopped
2 fennel bulbs, very finely sliced, some
    leaves reserved for garnish
2½ tsp cumin seeds, toasted in a dry pan
¼ cup favourite vinaigrette
1 tsp ground sea salt
Freshly ground black pepper
5 tbsp extra-virgin olive oil
Splash of flavoured vinegar (optional)
Juice of 1 lemon + zest for garnishing
½ cup Greek yoghurt (optional)
Good pinch of sumac (optional)

Boil the beetroot in plenty of water until tender, about 40–50 minutes. Once cooked, drain and slip off the skins. Once cool enough to handle, grate the beetroot.

Combine the beetroot, half of the sliced figs, herbs, cumin seeds and one of the sliced fennel bulbs in a bowl together with the vinaigrette and lemon juice, and mix together gently with two wooden spoons. Season with salt and black pepper. You might want to add a little splash of flavoured vinegar at this point or a teaspoon of honey. Pile on a platter and scatter over the remaining sliced fennel bulb. If using, drizzle or blob the Greek yoghurt on top. Garnish with sumac, lemon rind, a few tendrily fennel leaves and the remaining fig slices.

If you can find beetroot sprouts, or micro leaves, these would be another fantastic garnish.

Serves 8

Almond Croissants

This is how we doctor our Almond Croissants! They work perfectly well with day-old croissants. Enough almondy attention fixes them right up! Top tip: these can be made ahead of time to be popped into the oven just before you wish to serve them!

Almond paste (frangipane)
130g butter, softened
½ cup caster sugar
2 eggs
1 tsp almond essence
1½ cups ground almonds
2 tbsp plain flour
12 croissants
½ cup flaked almonds
3 tbsp icing sugar, for dusting

To make the almond paste, beat the butter and sugar in the bowl of an electric mixer until pale and creamy. Beat in egg and almond essence. Stir in ground almonds and flour.

Heat oven to 180°C. Slice the croissants in half lengthways, not all the way through. With a broad butter knife or spreader, slather the bottom half of the croissant with almond paste. Spread some more paste on top of the croissants and then scatter with the flaked almonds. We find that the almonds tend to fall off easily, defeating our ploy to almondify them, so we have to half-plaster half-spike them into the almond paste to make the almonds stay.

Bake for 10–15 minutes until golden. But watch very carefully – it's heart-breaking if you burn these! And they bake quickly! Dust with icing sugar before serving.

Makes 12

REG DES 85464   DESIGNED IN AUSTRALIA

Vietnamese Slaw

Clustered around the Metro Station in Arlington, Virginia, across the Potomac from Washington, D.C., is a little clutch of Vietnamese restaurants, a kind of Little Vietnam. It was here, during my time in the States, that I was first introduced to the marvellous fresh flavours of Vietnamese cooking. What a revelation! This salad will pull any meal back from the brink of dullness! Colourful, zingy and fresh, guests will welcome its joyful rescue!

3 large carrots, julienned
½ white onion, finely soliced
½ red onion, finely sliced
100g bean sprouts
½ white cabbage, finely shredded
¼ red cabbage, finely shredded
20g basil, shredded (optional)
30g fresh mint leaves, shredded
30g fresh coriander, roughly chopped

Dressing

4 tbsp fish sauce
½ cup water
6 tbsp caster sugar
4 tbsp lime juice
4 tbsp rice vinegar
2 garlic cloves, crushed
2 tsp salt

Garnish

½ cup crushed roasted peanuts
1 onion, sliced in rings, tossed in flour
   and deep fried til crisp (optional)

Whisk the dressing ingredients together in a small bowl. Combine all the salad ingredients, including the herbs and the sprouts, and present on a salad platter or in a wide salad bowl. Top with the peanuts and crispy onion.

Serves 8

Satay Lentils

This dressing is such a good one, you might find all kinds of ways to employ it. And you will be amazed at how well it goes with nutty lentils and fresh greens. You could also add any blanched greens to this recipe – fine beans, mangetouts, pak choi, and a handful of fresh baby spinach.

300g lentils
Salt and black pepper
20g coriander, chopped
20g mint, sliced
1 head broccoli
300g frozen peas
1 tbsp white and black sesame
    seeds, toasted

Dressing
2 tbsp yellow curry paste
1½ cups peanut butter
½–1 cup boiling water
3 tbsp palm sugar
2 tsp fish sauce
¼ cup vegetable oil

Make the dressing by blending the dressing ingredients together in a deep container using a whisk or a handheld blender.

Cook the lentils in plenty of boiling water until just tender, about 10 minutes. Drain and rinse in a colander to stop the cooking process. Toss the lentils with salt and black pepper. Add a cup of the dressing and toss to coat. Stir in half of the coriander and mint.

Cut the broccoli into florets and blanch in plenty of boiling water for 3 minutes, rinsing with cold water to stop the cooking process. Blanch the frozen peas. Rinse, drain and set aside.

Layer the greens on top of the lentils: first the peas, and then the broccoli. Garnish with the remaining coriander and mint and a sprinkling of toasted white and black sesame seeds.

Serves 8

Geri's Seedy Waldorf

Once I have made a recipe a few times, it is usually adopted by one of the team in the kitchen. It is interesting how different cooks gravitate towards different textures and flavours and embrace them as their own. In preparing this recipe book, I had to sidle up to one of my accomplished cooks with clipboard in hand and say, "How do we make this salad again?" This Seedy Waldorf is so pretty and it has become Geraldine's own.

2 tbsp lemon juice
5 Granny Smith apples, cored
5 celery stalks with leaves,
    thoroughly washed
120g cheddar cheese
¾ cup sultanas
30g watercress
4 tbsp sunflower seeds, toasted
4 tbsp pumpkin seeds, toasted
1 tbsp linseeds

Dressing
¼ cup mayonnaise
5 tbsp Greek yoghurt
2 tbsp lemon juice
Grated rind of 2 lemons
Salt and pepper to taste

Whisk the dressing ingredients together in a small bowl.
To make the salad, cut the apple into slices 2 mm thick and then into julienned strips. Place these into the bowl with the lemon juice and toss a little to prevent the apple from browning.
Cut the celery into long thin diagonal slices. Cut the cheddar into ½-cm squares or julienned slices.
In a large mixing bowl, toss the apple, celery, and sultanas together with enough dressing to coat without making the chopped salad too soggy. Arrange the salad on a serving platter, adding the watercress and celery leaves into the pile here and there so that the leaves do not take on too much dressing. Scatter the seeds over the whole salad. You can also add extra sultanas if you like.
Serves 8

Teriyaki Sweet Potatoes

Dark and sticky sweet potatoes could be just the foil you need beside cool crisp salads. They are unfailingly popular in The Kitchen.

1½ kg sweet potatoes (red, orange
    or white)
¼ cup vegetable oil for roasting
2 handfuls baby spinach leaves
Toasted sesame seeds

Dressing
¼ cup teriyaki sauce
4 tbsp fig jam (not green fig preserve)
    or honey
1 tbsp Indonesian sweet soya sauce
½ red chilli, seeded and very
    finely sliced
1 tbsp lime juice
1 tsp sesame oil (optional)

Scrub the sweet potatoes and cut into 2½-cm chunks. In a large bowl, toss in the vegetable oil and then spread out in a single layer on a large, shallow baking tray lined with baking paper. Roast at 220°C for 25–35 minutes until the cubes are browned on the outside and soft in the centre.
Combine the dressing ingredients in a large mixing bowl and gently toss the sweet potato in the dressing to coat.
Put the handfuls of baby spinach on the base of a serving platter, spoon the sticky sweet potatoes on top and sprinkle generously with the toasted sesame seeds.
Serves 8

Black-Eyed Beans with Swiss Chard & Tahini

This warm dish is an excellent way to eat both Swiss chard and black-eyed beans. It can be served with flat bread or fragrant rice and makes a great accompaniment to simple roast chicken or lamb.

300g black-eyed beans, soaked overnight

1 kg Swiss chard, thoroughly washed

1¾ cups vegetable stock

½–¾ cup tahini

4 leeks, washed, trimmed and chopped

Olive oil, for cooking

6 cloves garlic, sliced

1 tsp ground nutmeg

1½ tsp chilli powder

1 large bunch coriander (about 40 g), chopped

Salt and black pepper

Lemon wedges, as garnish

Cook the beans in plenty of boiling water for about 40 minutes or until tender, then drain them in a colander.

While the beans are cooking, prepare the chard: separate the leaves and the stalks. Then chop the leaves roughly and the stalks more finely.

Pour a little hot stock on to the tahina in a bowl, whisk thoroughly and tip it back into the rest of the stock, and whisk again.

Fry the leeks in olive oil for 3–4 minutes and add the garlic. Stir fry for a minute and then add the chard stalks. Cook for another 2 minutes and then add the chard leaves, spices and coriander. Stir well for a few moments and then add the cooked beans.

Pour the tahini stock mixture over the beans and chard, season to taste and allow to bubble gently for about 4–5 minutes. If you find the sauce has thickened too much, you could add another ½ cup boiling water to thin it to your liking. Serve with lemon wedges.

Serves 8

Aubergines with Tamarind & Mango

This dish presents the kind of play on flavours that we relish! If you find the sliced mango too shocking, purée the mango into the sauce to create a very different sweet-and-sour note. These Tamarind Aubergines would be delicious with Koshieri Rice Pilav.

5 large aubergines, cut into 1.5-cm rounds

Vegetable oil, for roasting

5 onions, sliced

3 cloves garlic, crushed

3 chillies, deseeded and finely chopped

1 5-cm finger of ginger, peeled and chopped

1 tsp ground cumin

1 tsp ground cinnamon

½ tsp ground coriander

½ tsp freshly ground black pepper

¼ tsp ground cloves

6 tbsp tamarind paste

5 tsp brown sugar

1 cup water

Pinch of sea salt to taste

Flesh of 1 mango, cut into slices

Start by roasting the aubergines. Brush the aubergine slices with vegetable oil. Do not be tempted to do more than one brushing of oil on each side on the apparently thirsty-looking aubergines. This will lead to sad and oily aubergines! Place the aubergine slices on a flat baking sheet lined with baking paper and roast at 190°C for 10–15 minutes on each side until golden-bronze.

Fry the onions, garlic, chillies and ginger in some oil until the onion starts to soften and become translucent on the edges (12–15 minutes). Stir from time to time to prevent sticking. Add the cumin, cinnamon, coriander, black pepper and cloves, and cook for another 4 minutes. Add the tamarind, sugar and water and bring to the boil, stirring well. Turn the heat right down, pop the lid on, and simmer slowly for another 8–10 minutes. Spread some of the sauce on a warmed serving platter and arrange the aubergine slices on top. If using slices of mango, tuck these in between the aubergine slices and pour some more sauce over the whole lot.

Serves 8

Carrot & Beetroot Salad with Toasted Pumpkin Seeds, Chilli & Mint

Beetroot salads have such an unfair advantage on the colour front. And this one plays so nicely with the other root vegetables for a real fiesta! Bring it out when you need a boost of colour and goodness. You could roast the beetroots in the oven wrapped in foil, and although they are superbly delicious done this way, they do take a long while to cook. At The Kitchen, we don't have this luxury! You could also add other root vegetables if you like, because the dressing will tie them all together.

800g small beetroot

500g small carrots, peeled or scrubbed

Bunch of radishes, thoroughly rinsed

4 baby turnips, peeled (optional)

½ cup toasted pumpkin seeds

Dressing

2 tsp crushed garlic

Juice of 4 oranges + grated rind of 1

4 tbsp honey

4 tbsp cider vinegar

60g fresh mint (40g for the dressing, roughly chopped + 20g for garnish)

1 fresh red chilli, deseeded and finely chopped

4 tbsp olive oil

Sea salt and freshly ground black pepper

Boil the beetroot and the carrots in two separate pots. The beetroots will take about 30 minutes, and the carrots 7 minutes. Blanch the radishes along with the carrots for 3 minutes. And if you are using the turnips, you could also blanch these with the carrots (3 minutes).

While the vegetables are boiling, mix the ingredients of the dressing together in a large bowl, adding salt and pepper to taste. You may want to add some more vinegar for zing. Whisk the dressing well.

Once the vegetables are done, drain them in separate colanders. Spray some cold water over the carrots and radishes to arrest the cooking process. When the beetroots are cool enough to handle, slip off their skins. You might want to use latex gloves to prevent your fingers being stained.

Now slice the beetroot into smallish wedges or rounds and slip them straight into the dressing in the big bowl. Slice the carrots into long, diagonal slices 2 mm thick and add them to the beetroot in the dressing. Reserve a few beautiful carrot slices for garnish. Slice the radishes or turnips thinly and add most of these to the dressing, again reserving a few slices for layering as garnish on top of the beetroot.

Arrange the dressed vegetables on a deeper salad platter, and layer the remaining undressed vegetable slices on top. Drizzle over the remaining dressing, sprinkle with the toasted pumpkin seeds and the remaining mint leaves.

Serves 8

Courgette & Fine Beans with Citrusy Tahini

Although I get excited about the relationships of flavour, texture and colour in all our salads at The Kitchen, the majority of salads are designed to be complete in themselves. They are designed to hold their own. Of course, it helps when the vegetables are super fresh and locally grown. Here is one such salad. If you can't find fine green beans, you will need to blanch bigger ones a little longer and slice them into 4- or 5-cm pieces.

6 medium courgettes

3 tbsp olive oil

250g fine green beans, topped

Juice of ½ lemon

1 red chilli, deseeded and finely chopped

Salt and pepper

80g mix of your favourite leaves or a
    rocket, watercress, spinach mix

600g of small tomatoes, slow-roasted,
    or semi-dried (see Spend-the-
    Night Tomatoes)

20g mint, finely shredded

Dressing

1 clove garlic, crushed with a little
    sea salt

4 tbsp tahini paste

Finely grated zest and juice of 1 lemon

Juice of 1 orange

1 tsp honey (optional)

3 tbsp olive oil

Salt and freshly ground black pepper

To make the dressing, put all the dressing ingredients together in a bowl and stir vigorously. It might look curdly and grainy but don't be alarmed – it will become smoother when you whisk in some warm water, 1 tbsp at a time, until you have a creamy dressing. Taste and season with more salt and pepper.

Wash the courgettes thoroughly and dry them with paper towel. Slice them into 3-mm rounds and fry them over high heat in batches, tossing and turning them occasionally until they are browned on both sides. Once cooked, transfer them to a bowl. Blanch the fine beans in plenty of boiling water for 3–4 minutes until just tender, then drain them in a colander and spray or dunk them in cold water. Drain and set aside.

Gently toss the cooked courgettes with the lemon juice, chilli, salt and pepper.

If your salad leaves are big, gently tear them into smaller pieces with the very tips of your fingers and arrange the leaves on a salad platter. Scatter over the dressed courgettes, the fine beans and the slow-roasted tomatoes. Scatter the shredded mint over the whole salad. Pull some leaves up through the vegetables here and there so that your salad does not look flat. Drizzle the tahini dressing generously over the whole salad.

Serves 8

Brussels Sprouts & Hazelnut Salad with Goat's Cheese

Brussels sprouts never featured much in my family as I was growing up and so I, unlike many of my white friends, have no horrifying memories of overcooked sprouts. This is a lovely salad to accompany a simple dish or as a beautifully plated starter.

½ cup hazelnuts, toasted and skinned

1½ kg Brussels sprouts (about 3–4 bags), thinly shaved or quartered with a sharp knife

4 Granny Smith apples, cored and sliced

3 tbsp extra-virgin olive oil

2 tsp salt

100g goat's cheese, sliced into rounds (or 100g Danish feta)

Juice of 2 lemons

Black pepper

Using a clean dishtowel, rub the bitter skins off the toasted hazelnuts and keep aside. Then, in a large pan or wok, sauté the Brussels sprouts and apples, and cook, stirring occasionally, until the Brussels sprouts are slightly browned on the edges, 6–8 minutes. (If you stir too much the sprouts will be overcooked and soggy.) In the last minute of frying, add the salt. Then add the hazelnuts, goat's cheese and lemon juice. Toss together and remove from heat and serve in a large pile with plenty of freshly ground black pepper.

Serves 8

White Bean & Tuna Salad with Parsley Dressing

The parsley vinaigrette dressing in this salad flecks the white beans with green and makes it, in my opinion, such a stylish salad. It's a quick one to throw together out of your store cupboard when friends have dropped in unexpectedly!

1 medium head of radicchio, cored, leaves coarsely torn (or a bag of "Sweet-and-Tangy" or "Italian" salad leaves)

2 cans cannellini (white kidney) beans, rinsed and drained

Kosher salt and freshly ground black pepper

Splash of extra-virgin olive oil

4 stalks celery, peeled and sliced thinly on an extreme diagonal

2 tins oil-packed tuna, drained and broken into large chunks

Juice of 1 lemon

Flat-leaf parsley sprigs, for garnish

Dressing

2 cups (packed) flat-leaf parsley (leaves and stems), washed and spun dry

3 tbsp fresh lemon juice

½ tbsp white wine vinegar

2 cloves garlic, crushed

½ cup olive oil

Kosher salt and freshly ground black pepper

To make the parsley vinaigrette dressing, pulse the parsley, lemon juice, vinegar, garlic and oil in a food processor and whizz until blended. Season with kosher salt and black pepper.

In a medium bowl, toss the torn radicchio with 3 tbsp of the parsley vinaigrette. Spread out the radicchio or the Italian salad mix on a platter. Place the cannellini beans in the bowl that has just held the radicchio and toss gently with more of the vinaigrette, seasoning well with salt and pepper and a splash of extra-virgin olive oil. Spread these out over the radicchio or salad leaves. Sprinkle over the sliced celery, and top with the tuna. Drizzle again with the parsley vinaigrette and a good squeeze of lemon. Garnish with parsley leaves.

If you use salad leaves instead of radicchio, go sparingly when dressing the leaves or dress only at the last minute. Radicchio is a lot tougher than a delicate rocket leaf, for example. This salad also does extremely well with a rocket base.

Serves 8

All Gold Chickpeas

I love this recipe. Gleaned and adapted from Hugh Fearnley-Whittingstall's excellent River Cottage Veg *cookbook, it is the equivalent of gourmet baked beans – only with chickpeas, and very mildly curried. Not only is it very more-ish, but you could serve it as a comfort supper with fragrant rice or even with artisanal bread, butter and bacon!*

5 large onions, thinly sliced

4 tbsp sunflower oil

1 8-cm finger of ginger, peeled and
    finely grated

1 tbsp chilli flakes (or to taste)

3 cloves garlic, crushed

2 tbsp curry powder

3 tins chickpeas, drained

2 cups All Gold Tomato Sauce or
    "Ketchup" of your choice

¼–½ cup water

Juice and grated rind of 1 lemon

Sea salt and freshly ground black pepper

1 large handful of coriander, for garnish

Fry the onions in the oil over medium-to-high heat for about 10–15 minutes or until they are soft and translucent. Stir in the ginger, chilli flakes, garlic and curry powder and fry, stirring for another 2 minutes. Add the chickpeas, tomato sauce and water to make the mixture nice and saucy. Simmer gently for about 6 minutes, and then stir in the lemon juice and rind. Add salt and black pepper to taste. Serve with generous amounts of fresh coriander.

Serves 8

Spinach Chop with Harissa, Almonds & Eggs

Nowadays we are so spoilt. Swiss chard and baby spinach come ready prepared in bags with little or no washing required. Although we often get ours from the gardens of Camphill Village, there's no shame in your saving time with spinach ready for cooking. This Spinach Chop would make a good breakfast or brunch for friends. You could put the spinach on a bed of yellow rice and do soft, poached eggs instead of boiled ones. To impress, drizzle with hollandaise sauce and a little chilli oil.

3 tbsp olive oil, for frying

2 tsp crushed garlic

1 kg spinach, washed and drained
    (or 2 large prepared bags of swiss
    chard or 2 large bags of baby spinach)

1 tsp harissa (see page 221) or chilli sauce

1 cup slivered almonds, lightly toasted

1 tsp sea salt

Zest of 2 lemons

8 hardboiled eggs, peeled and
    roughly chopped

3 tsp dukkah or toasted spiced seed mix

¼ tsp sweet smoked paprika

Add the olive oil and garlic to a pan and cook over medium heat until the garlic just begins to colour, but does not burn. Quickly add the spinach and stir fry until just wilted.

Remove from the heat and stir in the harissa, almonds, salt, lemon zest and half of the chopped egg. Place on a serving dish, and garnish with the remaining boiled eggs, chopped, and more toasted almonds. Top with a dusting of dukkah or seeds and sweet smoked paprika.

Serves 8

Tunisian Chicken

Confession 1: I have never been wild about Peppadews. But for this recipe I push past my prejudice and embrace their distinct flavour and colour. Confession 2: In truth, I think this recipe has little to do with Tunisia.

Marinade

½ cup raisins

1 cup Peppadews + ½ cup of the juice
    from the jar

2 large red peppers, roasted whole,
    peeled and seeded

2 tbsp hot chutney (optional)

Sea salt and white pepper

8 chicken breasts, deboned, with skin on

¼ cup vegetable oil

Jewelled Relish

½ cup currants

½ cup pitted green olives

½ cup Peppadews, finely chopped

¼ cup extra-virgin olive oil

¼ cup sherry vinegar

½ tsp sea salt

For the chicken marinade, plump up the raisins by placing them in a bowl and adding ½ cup warm water. This should take about 10 minutes.

Then put the raisins, the Peppadews, their juice and the peeled roasted peppers and salt in a food processor and purée until smooth. If you are partial to more heat, you could add hot chutney to the purée.

Season the chicken breasts with salt and white pepper and pour the peppadew purée over the chicken breasts, turning briefly to coat, and leave to marinate for at least 30 minutes or up to 4 hours.

To make the relish, add all the jewelled bits together with the olive oil, sherry vinegar and salt in a small bowl.

When you are ready to cook the chicken, pre-heat the oven to 180°C. Lay out the peppadewed chicken breasts in a roasting tray and bake for 20 minutes at 180°C. Remove from the oven and switch the oven to grill. Grill for a further 6–10 minutes to let the breasts colour beautifully.

Serve the breasts lavished with relish jewels on top. This recipe also works very well with Chicken Skewers – like jewelled sosaties!

Serves 8

Chocolate Buttermilk Cake

The buttermilk in this cake makes for a moist and delectable sponge. We do it in two layers but you could truly impress with four layers sandwiched together with chocolate pecan icing. A classic chocolate cake.

Non-stick vegetable oil cooking spray

3¼ cups cake flour

1 cup cocoa powder

1½ tsp baking soda

1½ tsp salt

3 large eggs

2¾ cups sugar

3 cups vegetable oil

1½ cups buttermilk

1½ tsp white vinegar

1½ tsp vanilla extract

Icing

½ cup + 3 tbsp unsalted butter

½ cup cocoa powder

½ cup milk

½ tsp salt

5 cups powdered sugar, sifted
   + more for dusting

1 ⅓ cups toasted pecans or walnuts,
   roughly chopped (optional)

Place a rack in the middle of an oven preheated to 160°C. Coat two 23-cm-diameter cake pans with non-stick spray, line bottoms with baking-paper rounds, and coat again with non-stick spray. Set aside.

Whisk together flour, cocoa powder, baking soda and salt in a large bowl. Set aside.

Using an electric mixer on medium speed, beat eggs in a large bowl until slightly frothy. With the mixer on high, gradually add sugar. Beat until mixture is pale and has doubled in volume, about 7–8 minutes.

Reduce mixer speed to medium, and gradually add the oil. Beat until emulsified (the mixture will resemble a grainy mayonnaise), for about 3–4 minutes.

Reduce mixer speed to low. Add the dry ingredients in 3 additions, alternating with buttermilk, and ending with dry ingredients.

Beat to blend between additions, scraping down sides and bottom of bowl as needed. Add vinegar and vanilla and beat just to blend. Divide batter between the prepared pans.

Bake until cakes begin to pull away from the sides of the tins and a tester inserted into the centre of each cake comes out clean, about 50–55 minutes.

Transfer the cakes to wire racks and allow to cool in the pans for 15 minutes. Run a thin knife around the insides of the tins to release the cakes, invert onto racks and allow to cool completely.

To make the icing, melt the butter in a large saucepan over low heat. Whisk in cocoa powder (the mixture will stiffen). Slowly whisk in milk and salt, then 5 cups powdered sugar. Whisk until smooth (icing will be soft). Stir in the pecans and vanilla. Chill the icing, stirring often, until spreadable, about 30 minutes.

With a long, serrated knife, halve each cake horizontally, creating 4 rounds. Place 1 round on a cake stand. Top with ⅓ of the icing and spread to the edges. Repeat with the remaining cake layers and icing. Chill until set, about 3 hours.

These cakes can be made two days ahead. Simply wrap tightly in plastic and chill. Allow the assembled cake to stand at room temperature for 1 hour before serving.

Serves 12–14

Wednesday

I love wood stock

The Kitchen
111 Sir Lowry Road
Woodstock
Cape Town 7925
Tel: 021 462 2201

Tracy - The Kitchen

From Istanbul to Woodstock

I spent a week in Istanbul with my sweetheart. We savoured the most extraordinary flavours conjuring centuries of Ottoman flair – and I wept at every meal!

Of course the diversity of flavour, a deep respect for the freshest ingredients and a concern for the origins of produce struck a chord in my Cape Town heart. Here were people I could relate to! It was perhaps the richness of their culturally diverse past that made me consider again our own history and the possibility of a new shared identity in food. Of course they have had centuries of practice, but if I look at the way we eat at The Kitchen – our "scandalous" selection of flavour on a plate – I think it something of a triumph for our growing South African identity. In our little corner of the country we declare: this is how we like it! We are excited about how flavours sit alongside each other. How they show each other off and make each other more interesting. And through shared meals around a table, we begin to discover our love of these remarkable flavours.

Gypsy Salad

It is the dressing that makes this vegetable salad captivating. The vegetables themselves are as colourful as a carnival and the salad is so busy that you'll need little else as accompaniment for a main dish. This salad is especially good alongside the Roasted Aubs and Roasted Chickpeas.

5 good tomatoes, diced

1 cucumber, partially peeled,
   seeded and diced

1 red onion, peeled and diced

2 carrots, peeled and diced

2 yellow peppers, diced

30g Italian parsley, very
   roughly chopped

Dressing

2 tsp crushed garlic

1 tsp sea salt

½ cup Greek yoghurt

5 tbsp extra-virgin olive oil

Juice of 1 lemon

¼ chilli, seeded and finely shredded

2 tsp ground cumin

Freshly ground white pepper

Put the tomatoes, cucumber, red onion, carrots and yellow pepper into a large bowl and toss gently. Then whisk the yoghurt in a separate bowl, along with the salt and garlic and the remaining dressing ingredients.

Arrange the vegetables in a shallow salad bowl and pour over the yoghurt dressing. The vegetables will be dressed as the salad is served.

Serves 8

Aubergine Cardamom Jam

When you're eating simply, having a fabulous relish on your table can transform the most monastic meal into something extraordinary. It is for this reason that I always take this jam along when we go away on weekends. It is seriously fantastic with almost anything. Try it on a roast lamb sandwich.

500g aubergines (about 2 large ones)
4 tbsp olive oil
200g fresh tomatoes (or whole, peeled
    tomatoes), roughly chopped
1 red chilli, deseeded and finely sliced
Seeds from about 15 cardamom
    pods, crushed
1½ tsp ground ginger
1 tsp ground cinnamon
Juice of 1 lemon
50 ml sherry vinegar
35 ml moskonfyt or pomegranate syrup
    (or maple syrup)
200g soft light brown sugar

Cut the aubergines into 1–1.5-cm chunks, toss with the olive oil, spread out on a baking sheet lined with baking paper and blast bake at 200°C for 20–25 minutes.

In a saucepan, over a gentle heat, cook the tomatoes with all the remaining ingredients for 10–15 minutes. Add the roasted aubergines and allow to bubble gently for a further 10 minutes until the mixture is soft and thick.

Pot in warm, sterilised jars, cover with discs of waxed paper and seal. Once cooled, this jam can be stored in the fridge for a week.

Serves 16

* Moskonfyt is a syrup made from hanepoort grapes found only in the Cape and make a good alternative to the pomegranate molasses. Another option is caramelised verjuice, which can be found in supermarkets.

Lamb Kofte

Traditionally, kofte and kebabs are prepared while the customer waits. A little fresh tomato, onion, parsley and sumac salad is chopped while your meat is being grilled and the whole wrap of lamb and salad lavishly soaked in meat juice is presented to you right there and then.

We love Lamb Kofte at The Kitchen, because they open up a host of salad opportunities. And of course, they are great on sandwiches with Mediterranean salads and slaws. Here are our kofte, as well as some Turkish-inspired dips and salads for a mezze feast.

500g minced lamb
1½ onions, grated
3 cloves garlic, crushed
60g currants
50g sunflower seeds, roughly chopped
½ tsp sweet paprika
¼ tsp ground allspice
½ tsp ground cinnamon
30g mint, finely chopped
30g parsley, very finely chopped
8 tbsp vegetable oil, for frying
Salt and white pepper

Combine all the ingredients together, except the oil, and season with salt and white pepper. Then shape into small meatballs, just smaller than a golf ball or flatten into not-too-thin patties. Fry the kofte in a griddle pan, a few at a time, about 3–4 minutes on each side until golden and cooked through. Serve with a yoghurt tahini sauce and the Aubergine Jam.

These are also exceptional on a braai. But watch them – they cook really fast! Squash them into a soft pita so that the bread absorbs the juices. Add Mediterranean bits of your choice, including grilled aubergines, sumac slaw, hummus or tzatziki, and pickles – great party food!

Serves 8

Roasted Chickpeas & Roasted Aubs

Unlike most of the salads from The Kitchen, this roasted, spiced chickpea salad does not really have a dressing per se. It really is great as part of a mezze-style meal alongside a juicier tomato salad (Gypsy Salad, Shepherd's Salad, Chopped Turkish Salad). It would also be good served on tiny plates with drinks and your favourite olives.

Chickpeas
3 cups boiled chickpeas
¼ cup vegetable oil
1 tbsp smoked paprika
1 tbsp ground cumin
1 tbsp ground coriander
½ tsp salt

Aubergines
4 medium aubergines
¼ cup vegetable oil
¼ cup olive oil

Assembly
¼ cup olive oil
½ fresh chilli or a pinch of chilli flakes
2 cloves garlic, crushed or grated
Zest of 2 lemons
20g flat-leaf parsley, sliced
20g mint, finely sliced
Juice of ½ a lemon

In a large mixing bowl, stir the oil into the chickpeas to coat. Mix the spices and salt together in a small bowl and then stir the mixture through the chickpeas. Lay the chickpeas out on a baking tray lined with baking paper and roast at 190°C for 15 minutes. Then remove the tray from the oven, stir the chickpeas to turn, and return the tray to the oven for another 15 minutes.

Cut the aubergines into 2-cm cubes and toss with the vegetable and olive oil. Spread the cubes out in a single layer on a baking tray (or two) lined with baking paper, and roast at 190°C for 20–30 minutes until golden and soft. You might need to turn these too to ensure they are golden all over.

Make a little flavoured oil using ¼ cup olive oil, chilli, garlic and lemon zest.

Using your hands, combine the chickpeas and roasted aubergines together with the lemon-chilli oil. Toss in the sliced mint and parsley. Then arrange in a pile on a platter. Squeeze over ½ a lemon for a little more zing.

Serves 8

Blue Cheese, Date & Pear Salad

This is a versatile salad, quite complete in itself. It is great to serve as an easy starter. And, yes, with melba toast for a little '80s nostalgia … Of course, you could style your own version of a light and crispy "crouton".

1 small bag of your favourite leaf mix
5 slices melba-styled croutons or 8 slices
  day-old bread, thinly sliced and toasted
4 pears, cored and thinly sliced
1 cup pecan nuts, toasted and
  roughly chopped
1 cup dates, pitted and sliced
150g blue cheese, broken or cubed

Dressing
Juice of 2 oranges
¼ cup olive oil
Salt and black pepper

Mix together the dressing in a small bowl and set aside. Then place the salad leaves on a platter, tearing the larger ones into more manageable pieces with the very tips of your fingers. Arrange the toasted croutons in between the leaves.

In another bowl, briefly toss the pears, pecans, dates and blue cheese together and arrange the mixture between the leaves and croutons. Dress with the orangey vinaigrette just before serving.

Serves 8

Lentil & Rice Salad
with Lime-Cumin Dressing

This is a fresh and fun rice salad. I suppose the lime and cumin create a hint of Mexican, but somehow I don't think this salad wants to be stereotyped in this way. It just wants to be fresh and free.

1½ cups lentils, rinsed

½ cup lime juice

1¼ tsp sugar

4 tbsp extra-virgin olive oil

4 tsp minced garlic

1½ tsp ground cumin

Sea salt and freshly ground
    black pepper

2 cups cooked brown basmati rice

2 tomatoes, halved, seeded
    and chopped

20g coriander, chopped + 20g
    coriander, picked into sprigs

1 red onion, thinly sliced

2 avocados, peeled and sliced into
    thin wedges

1 lime, cut into wedges, for garnish

Cook the lentils in plenty of boiling water until just tender, about 11 minutes. Then whisk the lime juice, sugar, olive oil, garlic and cumin in a small bowl. Season the dressing to taste with salt and pepper.

In a large bowl, combine the cooled lentils, rice, tomato, chopped coriander and onion. Pour over the dressing and gently mix to coat well. Season to taste with more salt and pepper.

Tip the salad onto a salad platter, adding the avo wedges as you go so that there is avo all through the salad. Garnish with coriander sprigs and lime wedges.

Serves 8

Mebos Chicken

Mebos is compressed dried apricot usually sold as little "tongues" or as fat discs (which you can then slice). My grand-mother used to keep a stash of mebos, bought from Wellington Fruit Growers in Darling Street, in her large oak dresser. But she did not hide the stash very well – the glass window on the drawer revealed the orange allure inside! – and I managed to steal a good many handfuls of the sour mebos coated with sugar. The mebos sauce we use (from Quality Pickles) is a spicy chutney made from this sour apricot. A hot-sour alternative would work too. You will recognise this recipe as something of a South African classic!

8 chicken breasts, deboned

Salt and pepper, to season

¼ cup Mrs Ball's Chutney

¼ cup mayonnaise

1 cup mebos sauce

Season the chicken breasts with salt and white pepper and lay them out in a roasting tray. Mix the chutney, mayonnaise and mebos sauce together in a bowl and pour over the chicken breasts. Bake the chicken at 180°C for 15 minutes. Remove from the oven. Switch the oven to grill and grill the breasts for another 8–10 minutes until they are browned and beautiful. If you do not have a grill oven, pop the chicken back into the oven at 220°C for the additional 8–10 minutes.

Allow the breasts to rest for 10 minutes before slicing and placing on a serving platter. Pour over the pan juices and serve.

Serves 8

Smoked Snoek Niçoise

When we were little, my dad would take my brother and me to the harbour at Hout Bay. We would sit amongst the boats on the beach or swing our legs on the quay, and eat fish and chips. On our way home, we would have to get some smoked snoek for my mom. In my flavour memory there is a deep connection between smoked snoek and sweet potato (soetpatat). Together with tomato smoor, these are signature flavours of the Cape.

4 whole onions peeled, boiled for
    6 minutes, cut into quarters

Pinch of dried thyme

1 kg red sweet potatoes, cut into
    1½-cm chunks

Oil for roasting

5 tomatoes, halved and slow roasted
    with olive oil, moskonfyt and salt

400g smoked snoek (I prefer oak-
    smoked snoek from Hout Bay)

300g fine beans, blanched

5 eggs, boiled for 7 minutes, peeled
    and quartered

½ tsp roasted masala or garam
    masala (optional)

Sea salt

10g coriander, roughly chopped

Dressing

¼ cup favourite hot chutney or mebos
    chutney (or similar)

½ red onion, finely sliced

20g fresh coriander, chopped

Juice and zest of 1 lemon

4 tbsp water

¼ cup oil

Salt and freshly ground black pepper

To make the dressing, stir all the ingredients together in a small bowl to form a chunky vinaigrette.

Carefully toss the onion quarters in vegetable oil with the pinch of thyme and lay them on a baking tray lined with baking paper, most cut sides down. Toss the sweet potato chunks with some vegetable oil and lay out in a single layer on another baking paper-lined baking sheet. Roast both vegetables at 200°C for 20–30 minutes until soft and a little frazzled on the edges. The onions may cook faster than the sweet potatoes, so watch that they aren't too frazzled.

Once done, spread the roasted sweet potato on a large serving platter. Arrange some of the roasted onions over the potatoes. Drizzle the chutney dressing over the roasted vegetables so that they all enjoy some of the love. Spread the roasted tomatoes out over the dressed sweet potatoes and onions. Layer the smoked snoek out over the tomatoes and drizzle over more of the dressing. Scatter the blanched fine beans over the snoek and arrange the sliced eggs over the beans. Season the salad with your favourite sea salt, garnish with roughly chopped coriander and sprinkle with roasted masala if you like.

For a starter with a Cape flavour, you could roast the sweet potatoes in rounds, and make individual salads, layering this salad on top of the creamy sweet-potato base. Scatter with fresh coriander and offer a lemon wedge for garnish.

Serves 8

Sweet Leeks

This dish is elegant in its simplicity, just the way we like it! It was inspired by the little dish of braised "sweet" leeks served as one of the mezze plates at Anatoli Restaurant in Green Point, Cape Town.

4 tbsp sunflower oil

5 onions, chopped

2 tsp garlic

1 tin (400 g) whole, peeled tomatoes

6 tomatoes, possibly past their peak,
    roughly chopped (or 6 Spend-the-
    Night Tomatoes)

4 tbsp sugar

1 tbsp lemon juice

1 tsp Worcestershire sauce

2 bunches of leeks (8–10 leeks),
    slit down most of their length
    and thoroughly cleaned

1–1½ cups water

4 tbsp olive oil

30g dill, chopped

Sea salt and freshly ground
    black pepper

Heat the sunflower oil in a deep saucepan. Then add the onions and cook, stirring, over medium heat until the onions become translucent, about 8–10 minutes. Turn up the heat and allow the onions to colour a little further, another 4–6 minutes. Stir in the garlic, and cook for 3 minutes. Now add the tomatoes (the whole, peeled tomatoes as well as the fresh, chopped ones), together with the sugar and the lemon juice. Stir thoroughly, pop the lid on and turn the heat right down. Allow the sauce to simmer and reduce for another 10–15 minutes. Then add the Worcestershire sauce. Once the sauce is cooked, allow to cool a little. Using a stick blender, you can purée the sauce at this point if you prefer a smoother tomato sauce.

Cut the leeks into 4-cm lengths. Put them in a deep pan (one that has a lid) and steam them over high heat with 1½ cups of water. Keep the lid on the pan to allow the leeks to steam. If your pan runs dry, you will need to add a little more water. The leeks should be soft in about 10 minutes. Drain any remaining water from the leeks and add the olive oil to the same pan used to steam the leeks. Brown the leeks in the hot oil until golden and slightly caramelised in places.

Pour the sweet tomato sauce into a warm serving dish, and then place the leeks into the tomato sauce – but do not stir. Season with sea salt and freshly ground black pepper, and top with the chopped dill.

Serves 8

Mustardy Mung Beans with Caramelised Onion & Nigella Seeds

We had already discovered this salad in one of Silvena Rowe's books but when a customer came in clutching a photocopy of the same recipe saying, "You have got to make this one!", we knew that it was a strong contender. Our recipe uses more mustard because I am crazy about that flavour and more onions because the beloved onion is at the heart of the most satisfying dishes.

300g dried mung beans,
    soaked overnight
4 tbsp vegetable oil
5 large onions, finely sliced
4 tbsp olive oil
4 tbsp red wine vinegar
1 tbsp English mustard
30g Italian parsley, finely chopped
1 red onion, finely diced
10 sundried tomatoes, finely sliced
Salt and white pepper
1½ tbsp nigella seeds

Drain the mung beans and boil them in plenty of water. Once they are on a rolling boil, reduce the heat and simmer for 20–25 minutes until they are just tender and cooked through. In a large saucepan, heat the vegetable oil and sauté the sliced onions over low heat for 25–30 minutes until soft and golden.

In a large bowl, combine the olive oil, red wine vinegar, mustard, parsley, red onion and sliced sundried tomatoes. Season with salt and white pepper. Add the warm mung beans and ⅔ of the sautéed onions and gently toss through the sundried tomato-mustard mixture with two wooden spoons so as not to mush the beans. Arrange on a deep serving platter and top with the remaining ⅓ of onions. Sprinkle with the nigella seeds before serving.

Serves 8

Spiced Butternut with Lentils & Feta

It is the spices and oil from the roasting of the butternut that makes this salad so deliciously simple. Lucinda thinks we should do it just so – without being tempted to add lemon or orange juice – and I think she's right! The mint gives it just the zing to lift it from its earthiness and the feta its rich creaminess.

300g lentils
1½ kg butternut or pumpkin, peeled
    and cut into 4-cm chunks
½ cup vegetable or olive oil, for roasting
1 tbsp ground coriander
1 tbsp ground cumin
2 tsp sweet smoked paprika
1 tsp salt
3 tsp sugar
¼ cup olive oil
Salt and pepper
200g Danish feta, broken into
    rough chunks
30g mint, finely shredded

Preheat the oven to 190°C.

Boil the lentils in plenty of water until just tender, about 10 minutes. Drain, rinse with cold water and set aside.

In a large mixing bowl, toss the butternut with the oil, spices, salt and sugar and lay out in a single layer on a baking tray lined with baking paper. Roast in the oven for 20–30 minutes until beautifully coloured and soft inside.

In a large mixing bowl, toss together the lentils and olive oil, and season with salt and pepper. Gently toss in most of the roasted butternut, together with every bit of sticky spice or juice from the baking tray. Reserve a few chunks of butternut for garnish.

Arrange the lentil mixture on a serving platter and dot the spare butternut chunks over the top. Place the chunks of Danish feta over the whole lot and garnish generously with the shredded mint.

Serves 8

Shaved Beetroot & Pear Salad with a Moskonfyt-and-Caraway Dressing

When we find a salad like this, we fall upon it with great fervour. The vegetables shine, the textures intrigue and we get to use one of our favourite ingredients: moskonfyt. If you can't get a jar of this unctuous sweetness at farmstalls, you could use honey, pomegranate syrup or caramelised verjuice.

3 beetroots, peeled and sliced very
    thinly, or shaved
1 cup crème fraîche or Greek yoghurt
2 pears, sliced very thinly
150g peeled butternut, cut julienne
20g dill sprigs or watercress leaves
2 tbsp moskonfyt or caramelised verjuice
1 tsp caraway seeds

Dressing
2 tsp toasted caraway seeds
1 red onion, finely diced
Zest of 3 lemons or 1 grapefruit
4 tbsp white wine vinegar
2 tsp Dijon mustard
¼ cup olive oil
¼ cup walnut oil
Sea salt and freshly ground black pepper

Toast the caraway seeds you will use for your salad in a small dry pan over medium heat, stirring regularly, until fragrant, 1–2 minutes. Set aside.

Then, for the dressing, whisk together in a small bowl the diced red onion, lemon or grapefruit zest, vinegar, mustard and 1 tsp toasted caraway seeds. Gradually whisk in the oils. Season to taste with salt and pepper.

Add some of the vinaigrette to the shaved beetroot and allow to sit for a few minutes to soften.

On your chosen salad platter, put a generous spreading of crème fraîche. Layer the beetroot with the pear, julienned butternut and dill and finish off with more dressing, the moskonfyt, the remaining toasted caraway seeds and a flavoured sea salt of your choosing.

Serves 8

Avocado, Lime & Basil Sauce

Not exactly Turkish and not quite guacamole either. Think of this as a chunky sauce, excellent with fish or chicken or as an accompaniment to a pulse dish. The addition of basil makes this an interesting, sophisticated "sauce".

1 cup avocado, pitted and diced

¾ cup extra-virgin olive oil

1 jalapeno pepper, seeded and
    finely chopped

1 clove garlic, finely chopped

2 tbsp coarsely chopped coriander
    leaves and stems

3 tbsp coarsely chopped basil leaves

2 tbsp finely diced red onion

2 limes, halved or ½ cup lime juice

Sea salt and freshly ground
    black pepper

Combine the avocado, olive oil, jalapeno, garlic, coriander, basil and finely diced red onion in a bowl. Squeeze the limes into the mixture and mash with a fork to combine, creating a lumpy green sauce rather than a smooth guacamole. Season with salt and black pepper.

Serves 8

Spinach Tzatziki

I find this recipe pleasantly "warmer" than the conventional cucumber tzatziki. This versatile tzatziki has fine colour, texture and flavour.

3 tbsp olive oil

3 cloves garlic, crushed

400g fresh spinach, cleaned and
    spines removed (or baby spinach)

3 tbsp lemon juice

300 ml Greek yoghurt

Salt and black pepper to taste

2 tbsp toasted sesame seeds

Heat the oil in a large pan and sauté the garlic, then add the spinach and cook for a few minutes until wilted. Drain very well, discarding the liquid. Allow the spinach to cool and then squeeze with your hands so that the spinach is as dry as possible. Combine the cooled spinach, lemon juice and yoghurt and season with salt and plenty of black pepper. Serve in a deep bowl sprinkled with the sesame seeds.

Serves 8

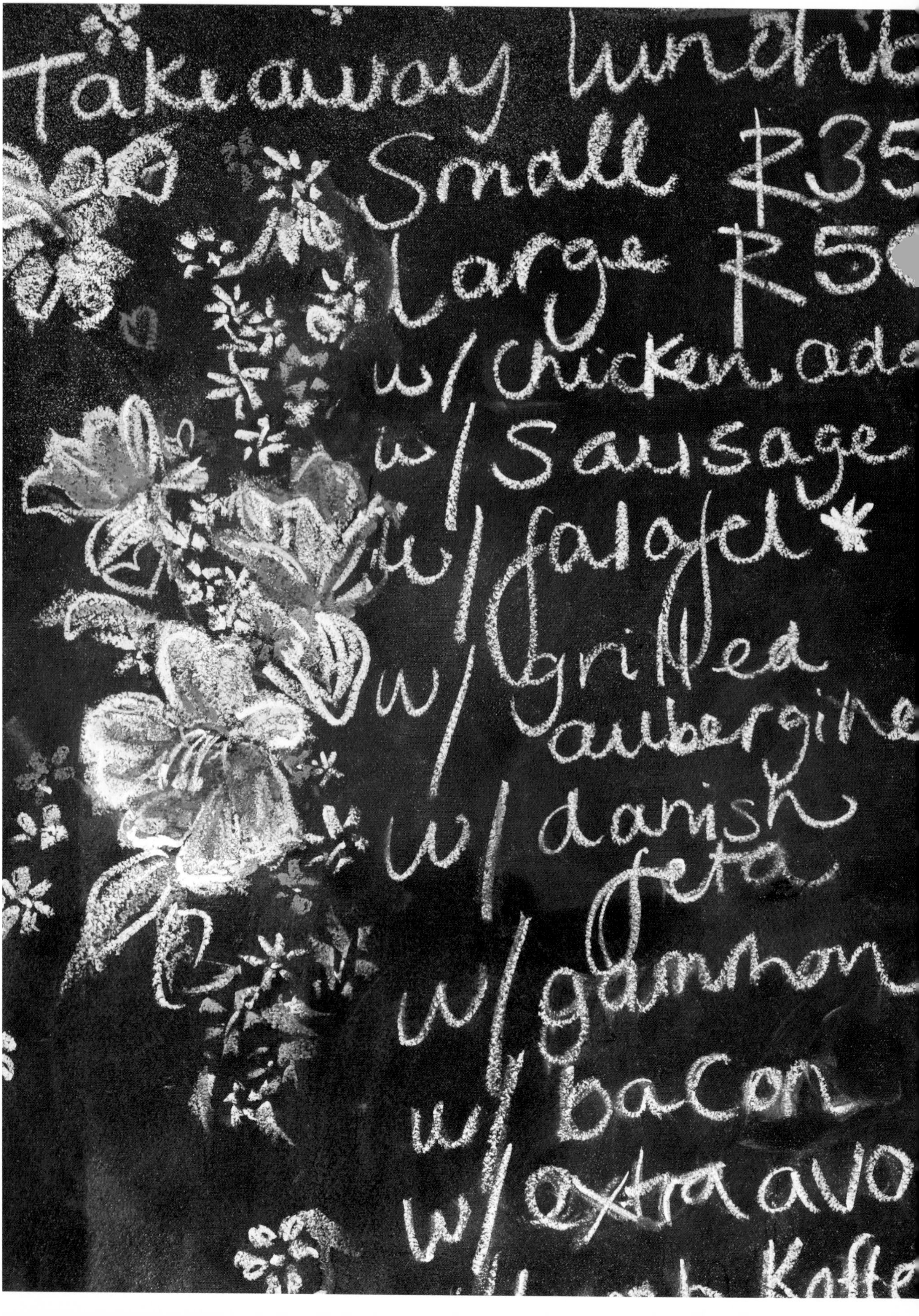

Takeaway lunche

Small R35

Large R50

w/ chicken, ado

w/ sausage

w/ falofel *

w/ grilled
aubergine

w/ danish
feta

w/ gammon

w/ bacon

w/ extra avo

Primavera Orzo with Peas

If you are going to spend the fat gram, and indulge once a year or once a month, this is the way to do it! This orzo is bad, bad good.

300g orzo or risoni pasta

12 medium courgettes, thoroughly washed and dried

2 tbsp butter

1 tbsp vegetable oil

750 ml cream

2 tbsp good-quality chicken stock powder

1 tsp white pepper

2 cups frozen baby peas

Salt to taste

Boil the orzo pasta in plenty of salted water for 7–8 minutes. The pasta should have quite a bit of bite, just before al denté, because we want it to take on the warm cream sauce. Drain the orzo in a colander and rinse briefly with cold water to stop the cooking process.

Slice the courgettes into rounds 2 mm thick and fry in butter and oil in a frying pan until golden. You may need to fry the courgettes in batches so as not to overcrowd the pan. Set aside.

Heat the cream in a saucepan and add the stock powder and at least ½ a teaspoon of white pepper and stir. When the cream has just come to the boil add the fried courgettes and frozen peas and cook for 3–4 minutes with the cream. Add the cooked orzo and stir through to coat. Taste and adjust seasoning. You might need more salt. This recipe is all about cream, stock and white pepper, so don't be too shy on the white pepper either. Pour into a heated serving bowl and eat before it gets too cold.

If you want to be even badder, you could add any one (or more) of the following:

100g chopped ham or gammon

700g spinach, blanched

100g of your favourite blue cheese

100g grated Gruyère or Parmesan cheese

Serves 8

Shepherd's Salad

In the back yard of the house in Genadendal where my father grew up grows a pomegranate tree. I stood wide-eyed the first time my father opened a pomegranate and I saw its jewels and outrageous coloured juice spilling onto the dusty ground. And as for the vegetables! My father uses his hands to demonstrate the monster size of vegetables from Genadendal: King Edward potatoes and Australian browns (onions). He and his father would bring them to market in Cape Town not far from where The Kitchen stands today. My favourite of the stories my father tells is how when he would come home for lunch his mother would give each of his brothers and sisters a packet of salt and send them back to school through the gardens to eat tomatoes on the way.

Here is a salad using simple vegetable ingredients and pomegranates.

2 yellow peppers, deseeded and diced

2 cucumbers, cut into chunks

1 green chilli, chopped

4 beautiful tomatoes, cut into chunks

1½ red onions, peeled and diced

8 radishes, thinly sliced

2 cups Italian parsley

5 tbsp dill, chopped

1 cos lettuce, shredded

½ cup pomegranate seeds

Dressing

Juice of 1 lemon

5 tbsp extra-virgin olive oil

Sea salt and freshly ground
   black pepper

2 tsp pomegranate molasses
   (or moskonfyt)

1½ cups cooked barley (optional)

Toss together all the ingredients, along with the dressing, and adjust the seasoning. Serve on a deep platter.

Serves 8

* Moskonfyt is a syrup made from hanepoort grapes found only in the Cape and make a good alternative to the pomegranate molasses. Another option is caramelised verjuice, which can be found in supermarkets.

Spiced Ginger Cake with Creamed-Cheese Icing

I have always been partial to spiced cakes. This one, with its unexpected cream-cheese icing, is particularly good. For a plainer tea cake, you could of course serve it without the icing.

1¼ cups cake flour

1 tsp baking powder

1 tbsp + 2 tsp ground ginger

¾ tsp ground cinnamon

¼ tsp ground cloves

¼ tsp ground nutmeg

⅛ tsp ground cardamom

¼ tsp salt

½ cup + 2 tbsp Guinness
  (or milk stout)

¾ cup Golden Syrup

½ tsp baking soda

2 large eggs (at room temperature)

¾ cup granulated sugar

½ cup light brown sugar, packed

½ cup vegetable oil

Icing

2 cups cream cheese

½ cup soft butter

1¼ cup icing sugar, sifted

Liberally butter two cake pans and dust with flour, tapping out the excess flour, and preheat oven to 180° C. Then sift together the flour, baking powder, spices and salt in a bowl and set aside. In a small saucepan over medium heat, stir together the Guinness and Golden Syrup and bring to the boil. Whisk in the baking soda. The mixture will foam up when you add the baking soda. Immediately remove from the heat and let the mixture cool to room temperature.

In the bowl of a cake mixer fitted with the whisk attachment, combine the eggs and granulated and brown sugar and whisk on medium speed until well combined and light in colour, about 4–5 minutes. Slowly drizzle in the vegetable oil and beat until combined.

Reduce the speed to low and slowly add the Guinness-and-Golden-Syrup mixture. Stop the mixer and scrape down the sides of the bowl, then return to low speed and slowly add the dry ingredients, beating only until combined. Remove the bowl from the mixer and fold by hand a few more times with the spatula. Divide the mixture between the prepared tins.

Bake until nicely risen and lightly browned at the edges, about 45–50 minutes. Transfer to wire racks and allow to cool for 20 minutes.

Wrap tightly in plastic wrap and refrigerate to ensure the interiors are completely cooled before decorating. You could do this for 1 hour or up to 3 days.

To make the icing, whisk softened cream cheese and soft butter together thoroughly in a standing mixer until very smooth and slowly add in the icing sugar. Use a spatula or palette knife to smooth the icing over the surface of the cake.

Serves 12–14

Thursday

Asian Potato Salad with Ginger Vinaigrette

For this Asian Potato Salad, the julienned potatoes are blanched briefly so that they are not raw but retain some of their crispness. It is an unusual salad, but I'm very fond of it. Mandolins are becoming very fashionable with the new regard for raw vegetables that we are experiencing in the food world. Just be very careful of your fingers! Or slice like we do at The Kitchen, with a good, sharp knife!

6 potatoes, peeled

4 carrots, peeled

200g brown mushrooms, finely sliced
(or 100g wood ear mushrooms, soaked, drained and rinsed again)

30g basil, chopped

30g mint, chopped

30g dill, chopped

30g coriander, chopped

Dressing

8-cm piece ginger (50g chopped)

2 cloves garlic, chopped

¼ cup brown sugar

60 ml rice vinegar

50 ml tamari

2 tsp sesame oil

50 ml flaxseed oil (optional)

¼ cup vegetable oil

Bring a pot of salted water to the boil. Then, with a very sharp knife, cut the potatoes into fine julienned strips. Blanch the potato strips in the salted water for 4 minutes, then drain and refresh under cold water. Make sure the strips have been well drained before adding them to the serving bowl or platter. Then, using a very sharp knife, cut the carrots into finely julienned strips. Add these to the julienned potato, along with the mushrooms and chopped herbs (reserve some herbs for garnish).

Make the dressing by blending the ginger and garlic in a food processor. Whizz in the sugar, vinegar, tamari and sesame and flaxseed oils. Mix in the vegetable oil.

Pour the dressing over the salad, mix gently with your fingers and pile onto a salad platter. Garnish with the reserved herbs.

Serves 8

Asian Avocado Salsa

Oh. My. Goodness. This salad is so delicious that we are almost reluctant to put it out in the shop. It creates a kind of frenzy. Once we start, there go all the avos! You will love making and eating this.

1 tbsp sesame seeds

3 tbsp rice vinegar

2 tbsp mirin (sweet Japanese rice wine)

2 tbsp Kikkoman soya sauce

2 tsp sesame oil

1½ tsp sea salt

2 tsp prepared wasabi paste

3–4 avocados, halved, pitted, peeled and cut into 2-cm cubes

6 spring onions, thinly sliced on the diagonal

5 radishes, finely diced

100g watercress, picked a little

Toast the sesame seeds in a dry pan over medium heat until aromatic and light golden, about 3 minutes. Transfer to a small bowl to cool.

Whisk together the rice vinegar, mirin, soya sauce, sesame oil, salt and wasabi paste in a bowl. Then toss the avocado, spring onions and radishes gently in the dressing to coat. Arrange the watercress on the salad platter. Lay out the avo salsa on and around the watercress. Sprinkle the salsa with the toasted sesame seeds.

Serves 8

Courgette Crumb Salad

The crumb mixture in this recipe can also be used to stuff grilled aubergines to make an Involtini, which can be baked with tomato sauce and a drizzle of strong Parmesan white sauce. In fact, this is how this recipe was born. How could we fail to employ the leftover crumb mixture? The walnut "raisin-ed" crumbs were calling to the courgettes!

7 medium courgettes, thoroughly
    washed, dried and trimmed
Stalks of 1 head of broccoli (or 200g
    long-stemmed broccoli), blanched
Olive oil, for griddling
2 tbsp butter, for frying
2 tsp chopped garlic

Crumb Mixture
1½ cups fresh breadcrumbs from
    artisanal bread
3 tbsp walnuts, toasted and
    roughly chopped
Grated rind of ½ orange
3 tbsp raisins or sultanas
50g Danish feta
2 tbsp olive oil
Salt and black pepper
2 tbsp basil, roughly chopped
1 tbsp grated Parmesan

Slice the courgettes into long, thin diagonal slices, coat them lightly with olive oil and cook them in a griddle or frying pan until lightly coloured on both sides. Fry or griddle in batches and set aside.

Slice the blanched broccoli stalks and toss them in a hot pan with butter and garlic until warmed through and fragrant, about 3 minutes.

Toss together the cooked courgettes and the fried broccoli stalks, season with salt and pepper, and arrange on a serving platter.

To make the crumb topping, combine all the ingredients together in a bowl except for the basil and the Parmesan. Stir fry the mixture in a large pan for 3–4 minutes until the crumbs are just golden. Add the chopped basil and Parmesan and sprinkle immediately over the waiting courgettes and broccoli.

Serves 8

Mushroom & Watercress Salad with Crumbs

This is a simple, delicate salad. Think light and think restraint. Choose the most beautiful mushrooms you can find from markets and supermarkets. I am lucky enough to have friends who bring me some of their harvest from the slopes of Table Mountain.

½ cup coarse breadcrumbs (if they are
  just a day old, they get even crispier)
4 tbsp olive oil
500g thinly sliced mushrooms
½ small red onion, very thinly sliced
  into rings
30g watercress leaves
Juice of ½ a lemon

Dressing
3 tbsp sherry vinegar
2 tsp Dijon mustard
1½ tsp honey
½ cup vegetable oil
Sea salt and freshly ground black pepper

Whisk the ingredients of the vinaigrette dressing together in a small bowl or shake together in a screw-topped jar.

To make the breadcrumbs, add olive oil to a deep pan and, over medium-high heat, cook the crumbs, stirring regularly until golden brown. Season with salt and pepper and your favourite seasoning and transfer to a tray lined with paper towel to cool.

Combine the mushrooms, red onion, and some of the watercress in a large bowl. Add the vinaigrette and toss gently with your fingers. Then arrange and spread out on a platter with the remaining watercress. Sprinkle with sea salt, black pepper, a squeeze of lemon and finally the toasted breadcrumbs.

Serves 8

Potato Gnocchi

It's just a theory, but I think that if you're a good baker, you would make good gnocchi. Like baking, they require a gentle touch and a patient heart. These are so easy though that they could make anyone look good!

1 kg potatoes
200g Danish feta
400g plain flour + ½ cup for your hands
2 eggs, lightly beaten
Sea salt and black pepper

Scrub or peel the skin from the potatoes, removing any blemishes or eyes, and then cut the potatoes into chunks. Boil the potatoes in well-salted water for 5 minutes, and then turn down to a simmer for a further 7 minutes until tender. Then strain in a colander.

Mash the potatoes – but not too thoroughly, or the gnocchi will lose its texture. Transfer to a bowl and when the mashed potato is tepid, add the feta, flour, eggs and some of the salt and pepper. Using wooden spoons or your hands, mix thoroughly and bring together to form a firm dough. Knead gently for a few minutes then roll the dough into sausages, about 1.5 cm in diameter. Dust your hands with flour to shape the gnocchi. Cut each one into lengths of 2.5–3 cm. Bring a large pot of salted water to a gentle simmer. Cook the gnocchi, in batches, for 1–2 minutes. As they rise to the surface, scoop them out with a slotted spoon and transfer to a lightly buttered warm dish. Serve with your favourite tomato sauce similar to the one on page 108 (with Sweet Leeks) or pesto, or with butter or olive oil and plenty of black pepper. Finish with chopped herbs and/ or finely grated or shaved cheese.

Serves 8

Curried Tuna Salad

Here's a great salad to please and delight, with just a hint of nostalgia to win over your pickiest friends. With a loaf of good bread and olive oil, you're set for a lunch!

1 red onion, finely diced
20g dill
20g parsley
1½ tsp curry powder
½ tsp sugar
¼ cup mayonnaise
3 tins tuna in oil
6 beautiful tomatoes, sliced
Olive oil, to season
Sea salt and black pepper
150g fine beans, blanched
6 hardboiled eggs (7 minutes)
Roasted masala, to season (optional)
Dill sprigs, to garnish (optional)

In a medium bowl, mix together the red onion, dill, parsley, curry powder, sugar and mayonnaise. Stir in the drained tuna and mix to combine.

Arrange the tomato slices on a platter in a single layer and season with a little olive oil, salt and black pepper. Then spoon the tuna mixture on top of the tomatoes, leaving a border of tomatoes to frame the salad, and top with the blanched beans. Slice the eggs into quarters and arrange these on top too. Season the whole lot with some sea salt and black pepper and some roasted masala if you like. If you have a few dill sprigs, those would also be a nice touch.

Serves 8

South-East Asian Mushroom & Red Bean Salad

In the last while, we have seen a growing move away from wheat and towards wholefoods and pulses. This suits us at The Kitchen perfectly. This flavourful salad is at home amongst blanched and roasted vegetables and leafy salads.

200g red beans or mung beans, soaked overnight
500g mushrooms, sliced
1 tbsp sunflower oil
½ small chilli, finely chopped
3 cloves garlic, crushed
1 tbsp mild curry powder or curry paste (yellow or sour vegetable)
2 tbsp crunchy peanut butter
300 ml coconut milk
1 tbsp lime juice (or more, to taste)
2 tsp soya sauce or ponzu sauce
30g coriander, chopped
½ red pepper, finely diced, for garnish

Boil the beans in plenty of water for about 30–40 minutes until tender. Rinse and set aside.

Working in batches so as not to crowd the pan, fry the sliced mushrooms briskly in oil. In your last batch, add the chilli and garlic and fry for another minute.

Then add the curry powder or paste and peanut butter to the last pan of mushrooms. Stir the mixture thoroughly and add the beans. Stir in the coconut milk and let the mixture bubble slowly for 10 minutes. You will need to stir regularly to prevent bits catching while the mushroomy bean mixture thickens slightly. Finally, stir through the remaining mushrooms and add lime juice and soy sauce to taste.

Pour into a serving bowl or deep platter with lots of chopped coriander on top and the finely diced red pepper for colour.

Serves 8

Aubs with Teriyaki, Pomegranate & Mint

This is one of the show-off salads that we do often for parties. We roast loads of aubergine slices (for big parties, this can take a while), and guests ooh and aah and make short work of them. A useful little number for your repertoire!

5 medium aubergines, cut lengthwise
   into slices 5 mm thick
½ cup vegetable oil, for roasting
¼ cup teriyaki sauce
4 tbsp fig jam (not green fig preserve)
1 tbsp Indonesian sweet soya sauce
2 tsp finely minced ginger
¼ cup pomegranate jewels
20g mint, shredded

Wash and dry the aubergines, cut off their "hats" and slice into slices 4–5 mm thick. Brush both sides of each slice with vegetable oil and lay out in a single layer on a baking tray lined with paper. You may need to roast in stages since absolutely no overlapping of slices is allowed during roasting. Roast at 190°C for 10–15 minutes each side until the slices are cooked, soft and golden.

Meanwhile, mix together the teriyaki, fig jam, soya sauce and minced ginger in a bowl. Then, once the aubergine slices have cooled slightly, lay them neatly in overlapping rows on a large salad platter. Here's a chance for you to be a little compulsive with presentation. Drizzle the sticky dark sauce carefully over the slices, and then sprinkle the pomegranate jewels and shredded mint over the glistening aubergines.

Serves 8

Jewelled Beetroot Slaw

I absolutely love this salad. Not only is it beautiful, but the wonderful play of the beetroots and caraway and the crunch of the cabbage make it a gem!

8 small beetroots
½ medium white cabbage, thinly
   sliced (about 4 cups)

Dressing
½ cup cider vinegar
2 tbsp Dijon mustard
Grated peel of 2 oranges
4 tbsp honey
¾ cup olive oil
Salt and pepper
2 tsp caraway seeds

To make the dressing, vigorously whisk together the cider vinegar, Dijon mustard, grated orange peel and honey in a small bowl. Gradually beat in the oil.

Boil the beetroot in plenty of water until cooked, about 40–60 minutes, and then drain. When they are cool enough to handle, don your latex gloves and slip off their skins. Cut the beetroot into thin slices and slip these into a bowl with a little of the dressing and set aside.

Use a very sharp knife to slice the cabbage into the thinnest slices you can manage. Then, in a large mixing bowl, toss the cabbage with the remainder of the dressing and the caraway seeds, and season with salt and pepper. Now very, very gently, toss in the beetroot slices a little at a time, plating up the salad on a platter as you do so. You want the effect of little jewels of colour rather than a uniformly glowing salad.

Serves 8

Chicken Medina

This recipe has morphed many times since I first spotted it in a Waitrose magazine eons ago and it has become one of our signature dishes at The Kitchen. The chicken breasts are marinated in harissa and tapenade and then baked with lemon and honey. Spicy-salty, sour-sweet. The overall flavour experience is bold and intriguing.

1 tbsp harissa (see page 221)
¼ cup tapenade
1 tsp turmeric
1 tsp cumin
1 cup chopped coriander
¼ cup lemon juice
¼ cup olive oil
8 chicken breasts, deboned, skin on
Salt and white pepper
4 tbsp runny honey
½ cup black olives, pitted

Mix together the harissa, tapenade, turmeric, cumin and coriander with the lemon juice and olive oil to form a paste. Season the chicken breasts with salt and white pepper and spread this paste over the breasts. Place the breasts in a baking dish, and drizzle with the honey.

Bake at 170° C for 20 minutes. Remove the dish from the oven and baste the breasts with the juices. Sprinkle the pitted black olives around the chicken. Place the dish back into the oven to grill or roast at 220° C for a further 8–10 minutes.

Allow the chicken to rest for at least 10–15 minutes before slicing. Garnish with some chopped coriander if you like.

Serves 8

Turkish-ish Koshieri

Of course this one's going to be good. How could it not be with all those crispy fried onions? Although koshieri is eaten in various forms all over the Levant, the addition of apricots in this recipe somehow makes it feel familiar to us here in the Cape.

300g basmati or jasmine rice
4 onions, thinly sliced
½ cup flour, for dredging onions
2½ cup vegetable oil, for frying
Salt and white pepper, and your
    seasoning of choice
2 tins chickpeas, drained (or 2 cups
    spiced roasted chickpeas)
1 cup dried apricots, sliced
½ cup currants
Zest of 2 lemons
50g fresh mint, sliced
½ cup pumpkin seeds, toasted
½ cup sunflower seeds, toasted
    (or pistachio nuts, chopped
    and toasted)

Boil the rice in plenty of water until the rice is cooked, about 7–9 minutes. Start with a rolling boil for 3–4 minutes and then reduce heat and steam gently for a further 5 minutes until the rice is tender. Drain the rice in a colander and rinse with cold water.

Slice the onions finely and toss them in the flour to coat. In a wok or a pot suitable for deep frying, fry batches of onions in hot oil for about 2–3 minutes until golden brown and crispy. Drain on paper towel, and then sprinkle with salt or your favourite seasoning.

Season the rice and chickpeas with salt and white pepper and toss in a bowl using two wooden spoons or your fingers. Add the sliced apricots, currants, lemon zest, mint and crispy onions and toss together. Arrange on a beautiful platter and sprinkle with the nuts and seeds and a handful of reserved fried onion.

Serves 8

White Cake with White Chocolate Ganache

"When shall we live if not now," said my favourite cookery writer of all time, MFK Fisher. Make this simple cake for a friend. It is a perfect cake to share with tea, but pile on berries and it becomes a great dessert. Seize the moment. Eat the cake.

100g plain flour
Pinch of sea salt
6 large eggs
150g caster sugar

Ganache
400 ml whipping cream
250g white chocolate,
    broken into pieces

Decoration
1 small punnet raspberries
1 small punnet strawberries

To make the ganache, bring the cream to the boil in a small saucepan. Pour half of it over the chocolate in a bowl and stir until the chocolate is almost melted, then pour the rest over and stir until smooth. Leave to cool, then cover and chill for at least 1 hour.

To make the sponge, heat the oven to 180°C. Butter two 23-cm sandwich tins with a removable base. Sift the flour into a bowl and add the salt. Place the eggs and caster sugar in the bowl of an electric cake mixer and beat for 8–10 minutes until the mixture is almost white and mousse-like. Lightly fold in the flour in two goes. Divide the mixture between the prepared tins and give them a couple of sharp taps on the work surface to eliminate large bubbles. Bake for 12–14 minutes until the sponge is lightly golden, springy to the touch and shrinking from the sides of the tin. Remove from the oven, run a knife around the collar to loosen, and then leave to cool. Each sponge will sink a little.

The sponge is so light and delicate (and easy to make) that this cake is most easily assembled on the plate on which you want to serve it. Loosen the two sponges using a palette knife and place one on a plate.

Using the rinsed and dried bowl of your standing mixer, beat the chocolate cream mixture until it forms soft but firm peaks – but take care not to overbeat or the cream will split.

Using a palette knife, spread a third of the white chocolate cream over the surface of the plated sponge. Sandwich with the second sponge and spread another third of the cream over the top. Use the remaining white chocolate cream to lightly coat the sides of the cake.

Just before serving, scatter the raspberries and strawberries over the top of the cake, mainly towards the centre. The cake itself should be served lightly chilled, but the fruit is best at room temperature.

Serves 12

Friday

Black Bean, Pear & Corn Salad

This salad has something of a salsa about it, but is far chunkier and crunchier – and the colour combination is superb, don't you think?

300g black beans, soaked overnight

Salt and pepper

2 large mealies, boiled (or braai-ed!) and
   sliced from the husk

2 pears, peeled, cored and
   finely julienned

2 carrots, peeled, and finely julienned

4 spring onions, finely sliced

30g fresh coriander, chopped

20g fresh basil, snipped

1 tbsp jalapeno peppers, chopped
   (or pinch of fresh chilli) (optional)

Dressing

3 tbsp lime juice

3 tbsp orange juice

2½ tbsp grated lime or lemon peel

½ tsp ground cumin

5 tbsp extra-virgin olive oil

Boil the black beans in a large pot of water until tender, about 30–40 minutes. Drain and rinse with cold water and set aside. To make the dressing, whisk the lime juice, orange juice, peel, cumin and olive oil in a small bowl. Mix the dressing into the beans and toss to coat. Season generously with salt and pepper. Add the julienned vegetables and chopped herbs and toss briefly through the beans. Pile on a serving platter.

Serves 8

Aubergine Stacks

Here's a little vegetable architecture for you. When you start building, there is no end to what you can do! You could turn many an aubergine salad into a work of art. This particular building is rich and delicious. These stacks are quite rich and you will need little more with them than some lovely greens and possibly a little barley or lentil salad on the side.

500g butternut or pumpkin, peeled
  and cut into 2-cm chunks
½ cup vegetable oil, for roasting
1 tsp cinnamon
3 tbsp sugar
5 aubergines, cut into 1½-cm rounds
20g mint leaves, shredded + picked leaves
for garnish

Sauce
4 tbsp mebos chutney (or similar)
4 tbsp mayonnaise
3 tbsp Greek yoghurt
1 tsp sugar
Salt and white pepper

Preheat the oven to 200°C.

In a large mixing bowl, toss the butternut chunks in ¼ cup of vegetable oil to coat the chunks. Toss some more with the cinnamon and the sugar and spread the chunks out in a single layer on a baking tray lined with baking paper. Roast the butternut for 20–30 minutes until soft on the inside with a nice, roasted finish on the outside.

Brush the aubergine slices with the remaining ¼ cup vegetable oil on both sides and roast in the hot oven for 20–30 minutes. Turn halfway through roasting time to be sure that both sides are beautifully coloured and the slices have a nice crust on the outside. The slices should be soft and creamy on the inside.

Whisk the ingredients of the mebos sauce together in a small bowl. To assemble, make a stack, starting with one slice of aubergine. Top with 2 or 3 chunks of roasted butternut. Drizzle with a 2–3 tsp mebos sauce and a sprinkle of shredded mint. Make another layer of aub, butternut, mebos sauce and mint, and finish with a third slice of aubergine. Garnish the stacks with the picked mint leaves.

Serves 8

Comfort Noodles

These are noodles you could make in a flash, and they are bound to hit the spot! The chopsticks you saved from your last Chinese takeaway are for eating these.

½ cup tamari

3 tbsp Chinkiang vinegar
   (Chinese black vinegar)

6 splashes of chilli oil

1½ tbsp sesame oil

800g Chinese dried wheat
   (or buckwheat) noodles
   (or 900g fresh noodles)

8 spring onions, white and green
   parts, finely sliced

If you have any these in your fridge,
you could add:

* 4 tsp grated ginger

* 1 egg per person

* sesame seeds or gomashio
   (see page 220)

* leftover bits of meat

* baby spinach or pak choi, stir fried

* watercress

* splash of ponzu sauce

Combine the tamari, Chinkiang vinegar, chilli oil and sesame oil in a serving bowl.

Cook the noodles in plenty of salted, boiling water until just tender, about 5–7 minutes. Drain the noodles, rinse them briefly and tip them into the serving bowl. Scatter over the spring onions and mix well. For a comfort supper, top with a poached or fried egg for each person.

Serves 8

Baba Ghanoush

As we closed for the Christmas holidays a few years ago, I was left with a box of aubergines and a bucket of Danish feta. And, in an unusually quiet shop, I put on some of my favourite music, and began the solitary task of burn-grilling aubergines on the gas stove. My heart was full of gratitude for my shop and my people and those whose lives I get to share in every day. I considered how small acts of devotion and care can have an effect so much bigger than we can imagine. This is my version of this Middle-Eastern mezze classic.

5 large aubergines

3 cloves garlic, crushed

½ tsp cumin

1½ tsp salt

1 tsp za'tar (see page 221)

Freshly ground black pepper

1 cup creamed cheese

¼ cup tahini

100g Danish feta

Juice of ½ lemon

20g Italian parsley

5 tbsp olive oil, for serving

Pinch of sumac, for garnish

Arrange the whole aubergines directly over the gas burner of your hob. If you do 2 or 3 per burner they support each other. To make you look like a seasoned pro, you will need some good tongs for this job. Leave the aubergines there on the direct heat, turning every 4–5 minutes. The aubergines steam inside their skins and the outside develops a great char-grilled flavour. You could, of course, do this on an outside grill but we like the urban ruggedness of our method! The aubergines should be very soft inside (you will be able to feel with a pinch of your fingers) after about 16–24 minutes.

Place the cooked aubergines in a colander, tearing the skin here and there (if it is not torn and charred already) so that bitter juices can run out. Leave for 30 minutes to 1 hour. Squash the aubergines again in the colander to extract more bitter juices. Then peel off the skin and place the soft flesh in the bowl of the food processor. It's a messy business, but try to avoid too many charred bits getting into your Baba Ghanoush.

Blitz the aubergine with the garlic, cumin, salt, za'tar, pepper, creamed cheese, tahini, feta, lemon juice and parsley into a dreamy spread.

Plate the Baba Ghanoush on a small platter, plate or in a dipping bowl. Drizzle with olive oil and sprinkle with sumac. Believe it or not, my friend Marcello and I even put Baba Ghanoush on sandwiches with rocket and toast them in our Dualit toasters!

Serves 8–10

Burghlers

These boemelaars have stolen many hearts at The Kitchen. They are terrific with our Hummus – and the crispy bits on their edges are the end of me!

1½ cup cooked bulgar wheat
1 cup cooked lentils
¼ cup flour
2 large onions
4 tomatoes, cut into chunks
2 carrots, peeled and cut into chunks
1 bunch fresh coriander
4 tbsp tahini
1½ tsp cumin
1 tsp coriander
1 tsp paprika
1 tsp chilli powder
Salt and pepper
Oil for frying

Put all the ingredients, except the bulgar and lentils (and the cooking oil), into the food processor and mix well. Season generously with salt and pepper. Mix the puréed mixture into the bulgar and lentils and shape with wet hands into burger patties or any shape that suits your needs.

Heat the oil in a wok or deep saucepan and fry 4–5 patties at a time for 3–4 minutes on each side. You might want to use a large slotted spoon for removing them from the oil. Drain on paper towel. Serve with hummus or any mezze accompaniment of your choosing.

Serves 8

Layne's Hummus

I once went on a road trip from Washington, D.C. to Florida. I think the trip was an attempt to salvage an ill-fated relationship. Layne, Jeff and I travelled in a vast, panelled station wagon borrowed from a friend. Our road food was Layne's hummus with carrot and cucumber sticks. I remember the Florida night air thick with the smell of jasmine. I was miserable. This hummus is the best thing to have come out of that time.

2 cans chickpeas, drained
   (¼ cup liquid reserved)
6 tsp crushed garlic
2 tsp cayenne pepper
2 tsp salt
½ cup fresh lemon juice
½ cup olive oil
¼ c tahini
paprika, sumac or za'tar
   (see page 221) (optional)

Place the chickpeas, garlic, cayenne pepper and salt in a food processor and purée, adding the reserved chickpea liquid and ¼ cup of lemon juice to smooth things along. With the motor running, drizzle in the olive oil and more lemon juice if you like. Add the tahini and process some more. This will pull the hummus together in more ways than one. Taste again and adjust seasoning. If you want a firmer hummus, add a little more tahini.

To serve, spread the hummus out in a little mound, shaping a little puddle for olive oil. Sprinkle over a few spare chickpeas and dust with paprika or sumac or za'tar.

Serves 8–10

Crispy Cauliflower with Capers, Raisins & Breadcrumbs

You may know that I am very partial to brassicas. This caper-raisin-breadcrumb mix is one that is often made with fresh baked sardines. I think of it as a gutsy Sicilian mix.

2 heads cauliflower, cut into florets
6 tbsp olive oil
3 cloves garlic, thinly sliced
2 tbsp salt-packed capers, soaked, rinsed and patted dry
¾ cup fresh, coarse breadcrumbs
½ cup low-salt chicken stock
⅓ cup sultanas
1 tbsp white wine vinegar or Champagne vinegar
Sea salt and freshly ground black pepper
30g Italian parsley, chopped

Preheat oven to 220°C.

Toss cauliflower florets with 3 tbsp of olive oil in a large bowl. Spread the cauliflower out in a single layer on two shallow baking trays lined with baking paper. Roast, tossing occasionally, until the cauliflower is golden and crispy, about 20–25 minutes. Heat 3 tbsp of olive oil in a small saucepan over medium-low heat. Add garlic and cook, stirring occasionally, until just golden, about 2–3 minutes. Watch carefully that the garlic does not burn. Turn the heat up slightly, add the rinsed capers and cook until they start to pop, about 3 minutes longer. Add breadcrumbs and toss to coat. Cook, stirring often, until breadcrumbs are golden, about 2–3 minutes. Transfer the breadcrumb mixture to a plate and set aside.

In the same saucepan, heat the chicken stock to a boil. Add the sultanas and the white wine vinegar and cook until almost all the liquid is absorbed, about 5 minutes. Remove from heat and set aside.

Transfer warm cauliflower to a serving bowl. Scatter the sultana mixture over, then toss to distribute evenly. Season to taste with salt and white pepper. Sprinkle the cauliflower with the garlic capery breadcrumbs and the chopped Italian parsley.

Serves 8

* To make your own breadcrumbs, allow cubes of ciabatta or other white bread to dry out, and then blitz them into coarse crumbs in a food processor. We do this a lot with the insides of our artisanal rolls. We also fry them in butter with ching ching, grated lemon rind, and a little chilli. These crumbs are tremendously useful to top anything from blanched broccoli to pumpkin. They are also the crumbs we use in our Mushroom Watercress Salad.

Crisp Cottage-Cheesy Kitchen Salad

My friend and neighbour Nazeem, from Woodstock Vintage, swears that the old Zerban's Restaurant used to make a cottage-cheese-based salad similar to this. I could not bring myself to include canned peaches, but I love the fresh crunchiness of this salad. The toasted sesame does extraordinary things with the cottage cheese. You could add alfalfa sprouts and toasted sunflower seeds and edible flowers from your garden.

4 cups cottage cheese

3 tbsp gomashio (see page 220)
  or toasted sesame seeds

3 spring onions, sliced on the diagonal

2 stalks celery, sliced, some
  leaves reserved

2 Israeli cucumbers, sliced on the
  diagonal (optional)

½ red or yellow pepper, finely
  sliced (optional)

3 young carrots, peeled and sliced
  on the diagonal

2 tbsp lemon juice, freshly squeezed

Splash of olive oil

Sea salt and freshly ground black pepper

20g mint, picked and sliced

Start by placing the cottage cheese in the middle of your serving platter. Season generously with the gomashio or salt and toasted sesame seed.

Sprinkle the sliced vegetables over the cottage cheese. First the spring onions, then the celery (and cucumber and peppers, if using) and finally the carrots and celery leaves. Sprinkle with the lemon juice and olive oil and season with salt and black pepper. Scatter the shredded mint over the whole salad and serve chilled.

Serves 8

Cos & Herb Salad

Well-dressed leaves are the cornerstone of a stylish table. This Turkish salad shows exactly what I mean, and can be a real asset. That little fresh bowl of green that enlivens plate and palette.

3 cos lettuces, outer leaves discarded

100g wild rocket

4 spring onions, finely chopped

30g Italian parsley, stems removed

20g fresh mint leaves, shredded

1 clove garlic

1 tsp sea salt

¼ cup extra-virgin olive oil

Juice of 1 lemon

½ tsp dried mint

Freshly ground black pepper

Shred the lettuce, then toss gently in a large bowl with the rocket, spring onions, and herbs.

Crush the garlic with the salt and whisk with the olive oil, lemon juice, dried mint and black pepper. Taste and adjust the seasoning. Toss with the leaves just before serving.

Serves 8

Root Vegetable Curry of the Seven Veils

I've always been a little embarrassed about my curries. Really good ones have such exotic mystique about them.
You just need to take a look at Reza Mahammad's Indian Spice to understand the breadth and depth of flavour. I am in
awe. Here is my humble take on a vegetable curry. In the glow of its inception, we imagined ourselves passing through
seven veils of flavour!

½ cup vegetable oil

600g butternut, cut into 4-cm chunks

7 carrots, cut into chunks

2 sweet potatoes, cut into chunks
　or wedges

3 onions, boiled whole for 6 minutes and
　cut into quarters

Seven Veils Sauce

6 medium onions, peeled and chopped

4 tbsp vegetable oil, for frying onions

2 bay leaves

3 cinnamon sticks

8 cardamom pods, crushed

2 tsp garlic, minced

3 tbsp ginger, chopped

1 tsp coriander seed

2 tsp ground coriander

1 tbsp cumin

2 tsp ground turmeric

1 tbsp curry powder

1½ tbsp vegetable stock powder

1 tin (400 g) whole, peeled
　tomatoes, chopped

¼ cup palm sugar or caramel sugar

2 tsp fish sauce

1 tbsp lime juice

1 green chilli, seeded and
　finely chopped

1 tin coconut milk

30g fresh coriander, roughly chopped

Preheat the oven to 190°C.

Start by tossing each kind of root vegetable (butternut, carrots, potatoes and onions) with vegetable oil to coat and roasting each on separate shallow roasting trays lined with baking paper. I prefer to roast the vegetables separately because some take longer than others and having them on separate trays allows you to roast them perfectly and with minimum fuss. The vegetables should take 30–40 minutes and be soft inside and well coloured on the outside.

While the vegetables are roasting, start on the Seven Veils Sauce. Sauté the onions in a deep saucepan over medium-high heat for 15–25 minutes. Stir from time to time to prevent sticking. You will really want to give more attention to stirring towards the end of the cooking time. Add the bay leaves, cinnamon sticks and cardamom and stir some more. Now add the garlic and ginger, coriander seeds, ground coriander, cumin, turmeric and curry powder. Stir the spices around to cook in the onions for 3–4 minutes. Add the stock, chopped tomatoes, palm sugar and fish sauce, and cook for another 5 minutes, making sure that the spices do not stick to the bottom of the pot. Once the sauce has thickened somewhat, add the lime juice, chilli and coconut milk, and cook for another 4–7 minutes. Taste and adjust seasoning. You may want more salt or more palm sugar or a drop more lime juice.

Arrange the roasted vegetables in a ceramic baking dish with the pointy bits of the vegetables sticking up. Cover most of the vegetables with the sauce, leaving some bits attractively exposed. Pop the dish into the oven 20 minutes before you are ready to serve. Garnish generously with the roughly chopped coriander just before serving.

The Seven Veils Sauce is particularly good with fish, but then reduce the palm sugar to 2 tbsp and add a star anise to the spices.

Serves 8

Red Pepper Lentils with Roasted Aubergine, Tahini & Za'tar

I first assembled this salad on one of those days when The Kitchen was particularly crazy and the girls in front were calling for more salads. We had filled up our salads three times already and still more people were filling the shop! I found some lentils ready cooked (blessed be!), the Red Pepper Pesto, and tore some leftover slices of aubergine, grabbed the remains of a leftover Tahini Dressing … and behold, a new salad!

3 large aubergines, cut into long
    ½-cm thick slices, each cut into 3
Vegetable oil, for roasting
300g lentils
30g Italian parsley, roughly chopped
1 tsp za'tar (see page 221)
Salt and black pepper

Red Pepper Pesto
5 whole red peppers
½ cup sundried tomatoes, hydrated
1 tsp crushed garlic
½ red chilli, deseeded and
    finely chopped
2 tbsp red wine vinegar
Salt and pepper
2 tbsp sugar
½ cup olive oil
½–1 cup water

Dressing
4 tbsp tahini
Zest and juice of 1 lemon
1 clove garlic, crushed
½ tbsp ground sumac
3 tbsp olive oil
½–1 cup water
Salt and pepper

Brush the aubergine strips with vegetable oil and lay out on a baking sheet lined with baking paper. Blast roast in a hot oven (220°C+) for 15–25 minutes, turning the slices halfway through until the slices are soft and golden.

Boil the lentils in plenty of water until just done, about 10 minutes. Drain in a colander and rinse with cold water to stop the cooking process.

To make the Red Pepper Pesto, toss the whole red peppers with some vegetable oil and lay out on a baking sheet lined with baking paper. Blast roast in a hot oven (220°C+) for 20 minutes until the skins of the peppers are a bit blackened all over. Place the peppers immediately in a ceramic or glass bowl and cover with plastic wrap. Once the peppers have sweated for a few minutes, the skins should slip off. Discard the skins and seeds of the peppers and place the gloopy peppers in the bowl of a food processor. Blitz along with the sundried tomatoes, garlic, chilli, vinegar, salt, pepper and sugar. With the motor running, drizzle in the olive oil to form a brightly coloured past. Slowly add the water to until you have a pesto with a softer consistency.

To make the dressing, place the tahini in a food processor, add the lemon zest and juice, along with the garlic and sumac. Process, adding the olive oil and water until you get a single cream-like consistency. Season to taste.

In a large bowl, season the lentils with salt and black pepper and a splash of olive oil and toss with 1 cup of the Red Pepper Pesto. Place the red pepper lentils in a serving platter. Arrange the aubergine slices in and over the lentils. Sprinkle with the chopped parsley. Drizzle with the dressing. Finally, sprinkle on the za'tar seasoning, some sea salt, and a grinding of black pepper.

Serves 8

Fatziki

Fatziki is a hybrid of fattoush and tzatziki. Clever, hey?

3 cucumbers, cut in half (or quarters)
    lengthways and sliced in 2-mm slices
    on the diagonal
1½ tsp salt
2 cups thick Greek yoghurt
3 tsp garlic, minced
½ tsp freshly ground black pepper
40g fresh mint, finely shredded
40g dill, chopped

Place the cucumber slices in a colander with ½ of the salt to draw out some of the cucumber liquid. Squeeze the cucumber a little and dry with a clean tea towel before proceeding to the next step. (If you think your salad is going to stand for a while, then it is best that you do this. At The Kitchen, we find this salad moves so quickly, that it doesn't really get much time to draw water and so we often skip this step.)

Mix the yoghurt, garlic, remaining salt, black pepper and herbs together and toss with the cucumber slices.

Serves 8

Parsnip, Orange & Date Salad

Think of this salad as a "composed" salad rather than a tossed slaw. Orange and date are such old friends and they play nicely with their new friend, parsnip. Trust Hugh Fearnley-Whittingstall, of River Cottage Veg Every Day *fame, to introduce them all!*

4 large oranges (or 8 small ones)
1 medium red cabbage (or 2 smaller ones),
    core removed and finely shredded
5 medium-sized parsnips, peeled and
    coarsely grated
Juice of a 5th orange
¼ cup extra-virgin olive oil
Sea salt and freshly ground black pepper
10 juicy dates, stones removed, sliced
5 sprigs thyme, leaves removed

Slice the top and bottom from each of the 4 oranges. Using a sharp paring knife, work your way around the orange, removing the skin and the pith. Cut out segments from between the membranes, working over a bowl to save every bit of juice and putting all the segments in a bowl.

Put the finely shredded cabbage and grated parsnip into a mixing bowl and add the juice of the 5th orange, the olive oil, salt and pepper, and toss the whole lot to soften the salad slightly.

Transfer the cabbage-orange mixture to a salad platter. (I am not an advocate of flat salads but this is one where the presentation does work well with a flatter look and you can admire the palette of colour before you.) Arrange the orange segments and date slices over the red cabbage and parsnip. Scatter over the thyme.

Serves 8

Fine Beans with Warm Curried Cashew Sauce & Topping

Inspired by Reza Mohammad, we have made this exotic, subtly flavoured cashew sauce to serve with fine beans. We think it very fine, particularly with its topping of toasty bits.

800g fine beans, topped
Salt

Sauce

80g cashew nuts + 50g toasted
    cashew nuts, for topping
3 tbsp desiccated coconut, soaked in
    warm water and squeezed dry
    (or 60g freshly grated coconut)
    + 50g toasted desiccated coconut
    or shaved coconut, for topping
1½ tsp turmeric
3 tbsp fresh ginger, grated
1 green chilli, deseeded
400 ml buttermilk
2 tbsp vegetable oil
1 tbsp sesame oil
2 tsp black mustard seeds
2 tsp cumin seeds
1 dried chilli (optional)
10 curry leaves
30g coriander leaves, roughly chopped

Blanch the fine beans in plenty of salted boiling water for 3–4 minutes. Drain and rinse with plenty of cold water to stop the cooking process. Leave for 15 minutes in the colander to dry. Put the cashew nuts into a bowl and pour hot water from the kettle over them and leave to soak for 15 minutes. In a food processor, blend together the nuts, soaked coconut, turmeric, ginger, chilli and about 5 tbsp of the buttermilk to make a smooth paste.

In a deep pan, heat the vegetable and sesame oil over medium heat until hot. Add the mustard and cumin seeds and the dried chilli (if using). Once they crackle and pop and the chilli has turned a shade darker, add the curry leaves and the nut mixture and stir fry for about 1 minute. Pour in the remainder of the buttermilk and allow the sauce to simmer for 3 minutes, stirring. Pour the sauce over the waiting beans. Top with the toasted cashews and coconut. Garnish generously with coriander. This sauce can be prepared ahead of time, and should keep, refrigerated, for 3–4 days. You could warm it up just before serving.

Serves 8

Macedonian Barley Salad

This dressing is a keeper. We don't want to fuel international tensions but this is essentially a Greek barley salad with the added richness of roasted aubergine. But you could do it without the aubergine and it would be good too.

200g barley

3 aubergines, cut into 3-cm
 cubes (optional)

¼ cup vegetable oil, for roasting

Salt and white pepper

1½ cucumbers, cut into chunks

Small bunch of parsley, very finely
 chopped (chiffonated)

30g fresh basil, leaves picked

300g cherry or rosa tomatoes,
 cut in half lengthways

1 red onion, finely sliced

1 cup calamata olives

200g Danish feta, cut into cubes or
 torn into chunks

Dressing

½ cup red wine vinegar

2 tsp sugar

1 tbsp crushed garlic

2 tsp dried oregano

1 tsp dried basil

1 tsp freshly ground black pepper

1 tsp salt

1 tsp vegetable stock powder

1 tbsp Dijon mustard

¾ cup olive oil

Blend the dressing together with a stick blender in a tall jug or litre bucket and set aside.

To make the salad, boil the barley in plenty of water until cooked, about 45 minutes. Toss the aubergine cubes in vegetable oil and lay them out in a single layer on a baking sheet lined with baking paper. Roast at 200°C for 20–30 minutes until soft and beautifully coloured.

Toss the barley with ¾ cups of the dressing in a mixing bowl and season with salt and white pepper. Toss in the cucumber chunks. Lay the barley and cucumber out on a serving platter. Scatter over some of the chopped parsley. Layer the roasted aubergines on top of the barley. Season with sea salt and another sprinkling of dressing, and scatter over some of the basil leaves. Now layer the remainder of the salad ingredients: tomatoes, red onion, olives and feta. Give a last sprinkle of dressing. Top with the last of the basil leaves and more parsley if you wish.

Any leftover dressing will keep well in your fridge for a week or two in a glass container with a lid.

Serves 8

Pumpkin Vetkoek with Moskonfyt

Something delicious happens when cinnamon sugar meets the crispy bits of the orange-tinged vetkoek.
The slight tang in the moskonfyt goes perfectly with these, as does a little melted apricot jam, honey or maple syrup.

240g (430 ml) cake flour
20 ml baking powder
2 ml salt
15 ml butter
125 ml milk
125 ml pumpkin purée
300 ml sunflower oil, for frying

Sift the dry ingredients together. Rub in the butter. Add the milk and pumpkin purée and mix well. Heat the oil in a deep pan. Test with a little of the mixture whether the oil is hot enough – it should start frying. It's also a good idea to dip your tablespoon in the hot oil before spooning the mixture, because then the dough will slide off the spoon more easily. Then spoon tablespoons of the mixture into the hot oil and fry on both sides until golden brown. Drain on kitchen paper and serve hot with syrup.

Makes 16

* This recipe benefits from a "drier" purée. For this reason, leftover roasted butternut and pumpkin work well.

Saturday

Lucy Pooler's Birthday Party

Lucy Pooler has style – oodles of it – which she carries in a sort of nonchalant, down-to-earth way. A great entertainer, she is famous for throwing a party! Providence shined down on us during the week of our shoot for this book. It was Lucy's birthday, and she agreed to let us cater it for her in her beautiful home in Green Point! With chunky walls, lofty ceilings, corners of treasures and an enviable kitchen, it was a dream location for photographing one of our parties! And Lucy was a most gracious hostess.

Spinach & Cheddar Gözleme

I stared, slack-jawed, at the sheets of filled savoury Börek and Gözleme pastries that sell by the kilo from shops in Istanbul. The shop assistant seemed appalled at the small amount I wanted to buy for our breakfast. Clearly, these are pastries that demand to be eaten in large amounts!

2 tsp olive oil
500g Swiss chard leaves, chopped
½ bunch coriander, chopped
½ red chilli, deseeded and
  finely chopped
1 red onion, grated
2 cloves garlic, crushed
200g cheddar, grated
2–3 sheets filo pastry
6 tbsp butter, melted

Heat the olive oil in a large frying pan and sauté the chard, coriander, chilli, onion and garlic for 2–3 minutes until the leaves have wilted. Remove from the heat, drain, and discard the cooking fluids. Cool in a bowl, then add the grated cheese.

You will need to cover the filo with a damp cloth while you're not working with it.

Butter one sheet of filo thoroughly. Lay another layer of filo over the first. Cut the large sheet into 3 rectangles. Working with one piece at a time, spoon some of the chard-and-cheese filling into the middle of one half of the large rectangle. Brush the sides with melted butter. Fold the rectangle in half to enclose the filling. Fold over the sides to seal and brush with more butter. Brush the outside of the rectangles with melted butter and arrange the "envelopes" on a platter. Repeat until you have 6 filled pastry envelopes.

Heat the remaining butter in a non-stick pan and sauté the Gözleme for 2–3 minutes on each side, until brown.

You can either keep the pastries well covered with a damp cloth until your guests arrive and fry them on the spot while they watch, wide-eyed, or you can fry them ahead of time and pop them into the oven on a roasting rack over a baking sheet to warm up briefly (3–5 minutes) in a hot oven. Slice into rough rectangles or triangles and serve immediately. These certainly do not last long.

Serves 8

Miso Broccoli "Brushes"

We've made this excellent broccoli salad many times at The Kitchen, but for Lucy's party I had the idea of making little broccoli "brushes" to mop up the heavenly Miso Dressing. This dressing has the power to enslave mortals. Be careful who you make it for …

Dressing

⅓ cup rice vinegar

3 tbsp yellow or red miso paste

3 large cloves garlic, peeled

2 tsp sugar

3 tsp chopped fresh ginger

2 tsp sesame oil

2 tsp soya sauce

¼ cup olive oil

¼ cup mayonnaise

Mix all the dressing ingredients together in a food processor.

For serving as we did at Lucy's party

2 heads broccoli

    (or 700g long-stemmed broccoli)

Cut the heads of broccoli into larger florets and blanch in plenty of boiling water for 4 minutes. Drain and immerse in iced water or rinse gently with cold water to arrest the cooking process and then slice the florets. Pour a puddle of Miso Dressing onto a tiny plate or into a bowl and place a broccoli "brush" in each plate to brush up the dressing.

For serving as a salad

2 heads broccoli, blanched

5 spring onions, sliced thinly
    on the diagonal

4 cups finely sliced spinach
    (or 2 handfuls baby spinach leaves)

½ cup roasted almonds, chopped

In a large bowl, mix the broccoli, spring onions, greens and dressing together using your hands. Arrange the "slaw" on a serving platter and sprinkle over the roasted almonds.
Dress this salad just before it is about to be served, because if it sits a while, it tends to discolour, and loses the effect of the verdant greenness you're after.

Serves 8

White Anchovy, Fried Crouton, White Bean & Egg Salad

I've seen marinated white anchovies in recipe books before and have always been drawn to them. We don't often see them here, though. When one of our suppliers said that he had some, I pounced. They are indulgent indeed. Not salty but delicate. If you see them in speciality delis, you should leap at the opportunity. That said, however, this recipe would also work well with good-quality "regular" anchovies – in which case, have lemon wedges on hand.

2 handfuls artisanal bread, torn and stale

Olive oil, for frying

2 tsp ching ching (see page 221)

Squeeze of lemon juice (optional)

1 tin white beans, drained

4 tbsp vinaigrette

Maldon salt and black pepper

1½ bags leaves (watercress, rocket, friseé are best)

16 marinated white anchovy fillets

6 eggs, boiled medium-soft

¼ cup olive oil

Fry the bite-sized torn bread, a handful at a time, with olive oil and ching ching. (I sometimes squeeze a bit of lemon juice on the bread too for a lively crouton.)

Toss the white beans in the vinaigrette and season with salt and black pepper.

Lay out ⅔ of the leaves, and sprinkle with ⅔ of the beans. Scatter most of the toasted croutons over the salad. Lay out all of the anchovy fillets (tear the anchovy in half to get 2 fillets). Break the boiled eggs with your fingers or, for a less messy effect, slice them in quarters and place on top of the salad.

Sprinkle over the remaining beans, along with their dressing. Season all generously with Maldon and black pepper. Garnish with the remaining leaves.

Serves 8

Felino Salami with Jewelled Artichokes

This is a great thing to do when you have an informal gathering and wonderful charcuterie. We used our favourite Felino Salami from Maurizio.

Salami

Slice the Salami on the diagonal with a sharp knife and arrange attractively on the largest wooden board that you can find. Slice your favourite crusty loaf in smallish slices. Position your best olive oil close by and a little bowl of rocket or basil or even Italian parsley. Then arrange the Jewelled Artichokes around your favourite cured meat. Encourage guests to get stuck in.

Artichokes

My dear friend, Tom O'Leary, nearly succeeded in luring me to work for his catering company in Anapolis, Maryland, over a decade ago. At the time, he was just embarking on building an empire of now-renowned Mexican restaurants and needed someone to take over the reins of his catering company. I worked with his crew for a few weeks and learnt a great deal. In the end, love called me back to Cape Town. It was Tom who showed me how to do these fantastic Jewelled Artichokes.

2 tins of whole artichokes, drained
½ red pepper, finely diced
3 tbsp finely diced red onion
1 cup black olives, pitted and
    finely diced

Vinaigrette
5 tbsp olive oil
3 tbsp red wine vinegar
2 tsp sugar
1 clove garlic, finely crushed
    with ½ tsp salt
1 tbsp chopped parsley (or oregano,
    dill or chives)

Slice the tinned artichokes in half lengthwise and arrange on a platter or on a board.

Mix the vinaigrette ingredients together thoroughly in a little bowl. Drizzle 2 tbsp of the vinaigrette over the artichokes and allow them to "marinate" a little while you chop up the "jewels". Gently mix together the peppers, red onion and olives. With a teaspoon or small cake fork, distribute the jewels in little piles on top of each artichoke half. Carefully drizzle over the remaining vinaigrette.

Serves 8

Date Pilav

This rice has such an exotic fragrance that I can picture it being served for the pleasure of a sultan. And the nut garnish is a revelation! But don't skip the step of washing the rice – this really is an important part of the pilav-making process: it removes excess starch from the grains. Slipping a clean tea towel under the lid of the saucepan when the rice has finished cooking absorbs the steam and leaves you with the desirable fluffy finish.

400g basmati rice
800 ml chicken stock
80g butter
200g dates, pitted and chopped
1 tsp freshly ground black pepper
½ tsp ground allspice
¾ tsp ground cinnamon
Pinch of hot paprika or chilli flakes
½ tsp sea salt
Long strip from a whole orange
30g shredded Italian parsley

Garnish
2 tbsp olive oil
½ cup flaked almonds
⅓ cup pine nuts
¼ tsp ground cinnamon
Pinch of sea salt

Put the rice into a large bowl and rinse well under cold running water, working your fingers through it to loosen the starch. Drain off the milky water and repeat until the water runs clear. Bring the stock to the boil, then lower the heat and keep at a simmer. Then melt the butter in a heavy-based saucepan. Add the dates, pepper and spices and stir briefly. Gently stir in the rice so that all the grains are coated with the spiced butter.

Pour in the simmering stock and add the salt. Stir, then bring to the boil and add the orange peel. Cover with a tight-fitting lid and boil for 5–7 minutes. The grains should all look plump and separate and the surface will be dented with little holes. Watch that the pan does not run dry. You might need to add ¼ cup more water to prevent the rice sticking and burning. Remove the pan from the heat, then slide a clean, folded tea towel under the lid and leave it to stand for 15–20 minutes.

To make the nut garnish, heat the oil in a small frying pan and sauté the nuts for a few minutes until evenly coloured. Tip into a sieve and drain. Sprinkle on the cinnamon and salt, and shake the sieve so the nuts are evenly coated.

When ready to serve, remove the peel from the pilav and stir through the parsley, using a fork to fluff up the grains. Tip the rice onto a serving platter and scatter on the nuts.

Serves 8

Tamarind Kingklip

One day, the Mount Nelson Hotel called ahead to say that we should expect a group of young men wanting to visit The Kitchen. Hamid was one of those visitors. Here was a man with a passion! I was riveted by his tales of Qa'tarian food and this dish, in particular, captured my imagination. The pearl fishermen of the Gulf would spend weeks at sea with only a few ingredients to cook with on their boats: rice, dates, fish and tamarind. They made a sweet, fragrant date rice and ate it with fish simmered in a tamarind sauce. Hamid's description of the recipe was far more complex than the one I have here, but I am hoping that it mimics the sublime flavours of his dish.

6 tbsp vegetable oil

6 onions, sliced

6 cloves garlic

3 chillies

8-cm finger of ginger, peeled
and chopped

1½ tsp ground cinnamon

2 tsp ground cumin

1 tsp ground coriander

1 tsp freshly ground black pepper

¼ tsp ground cloves

½ block tamarind paste (or ½ cup
tamarind paste from a jar)

3 tbsp brown sugar

2–2½ cups water

5 soft tomatoes, chopped

2 kg kingklip (or kabeljou),
cut into portions

1 cup flour, seasoned with salt and
white pepper or fish spice

3 tbsp butter

30g coriander, roughly chopped

Heat 3 tbsp of the vegetable oil in a saucepan and add the onions, garlic, chillies and ginger, and fry until the onion starts to soften and becomes translucent on the edges, about 12–15 minutes. Stir from time to time to prevent sticking. Add the cinnamon, cumin, coriander, black pepper and cloves, and cook for another 4 minutes. Add the tamarind, sugar and water and bring to the boil, stirring well. After 4 minutes, add the chopped tomatoes and simmer for a further 8–12 minutes until the sauce has thickened. While the sauce is cooking, lightly coat the pieces of fish in the seasoned flour. Fry the fish pieces in the butter and the remaining 3 tbsp vegetable oil until golden brown and cooked through, about 5–7 minutes.

To serve, plate the fish on a deep serving platter and spoon over the warm sauce. You could also place the fish on top of the Date Pilav (see page 204) and then spoon over the tamarind sauce. Garnish generously with roughly chopped coriander.

Serves 8

* On our way back from Turkey, we spent a night in Doha, Qa'tar, where we were met by Hamid, this time in full traditional garb, who gave us a fascinating tour of the city. We visited the souk, shared a meal, and when he dropped us back at our hotel, handed me kilograms of dates (some to cook with, some to eat) and – treasure! – a jar of his mother's own spice mix.

Middle-Eastern Tower of Roasted Aubergines with Yoghurt

The idea for this recipe comes from Sally Butcher's fabulous Veggiestan cookbook. I love assembling the tower. It provides pause to consider those for whom you are assembling it and an opportunity to bless them with something beautiful.

6 medium-sized (preferably long
   and thinner) aubergines
½ cup olive oil, for roasting
½ cup vegetable oil, for roasting
30g fresh mint, chopped
1–2 tsp za'tar (see page 221),
   for sprinkling

Sauce
2 large onions, chopped
2 tbsp vegetable oil, for frying
3 tsp ginger, grated
1 tsp curry powder
2 tins tomatoes, roughly chopped
2 tbsp sugar
Salt and white pepper
30g coriander, chopped

Yoghurt
3 cups thick Greek yoghurt
3 tbsp lemon juice
6 cloves garlic, minced
Salt and black pepper
Preheat the oven to 200°C.

Slice the aubergines into slices about 1½ cm thick. If you are concerned about their bitterness, sprinkle them with coarse salt and leave for 30 minutes to draw out bitter juices. Rinse and dry the slices and then brush them with the mixed oils. Lay them out in a single layer on a baking sheet lined with baking pape. Roast for 25–35 minutes, turning halfway through to be sure the slices are browned on both sides and soft in the middle.

To make the sauce, fry the chopped onion over medium heat in a wide, deep pan until golden and translucent, about 10–14 minutes. Add the ginger and curry powder, and cook for another 3 minutes. Add the chopped tomatoes, sugar, salt and pepper, and cook for another 15–20 minutes over low heat until the sauce has reduced. Add the coriander and cook for a further 5 minutes.

Mix the yoghurt ingredients together in a bowl and season to taste with salt and pepper.

Spread out a layer of aubergine slices on your serving platter. Spoon the tomato sauce generously over the slices. Then spoon the flavoured yoghurt over the tomato sauce, leaving bits of aubergine slice revealed so that you see the constitution of the tower. Scatter the chopped mint over the yoghurt and sprinkle on some za'tar. Continue with your construction, adding more layers of aubergine and finishing with yoghurt on the top, seasoned again with mint leaves and za'tar. Then serve with rice or naan or other flat bread, or even buttered couscous.

Serves 8

Vegetably Lentils

Vegetably Lentils, cooked al dente, are the perfect accompaniment to a rich roast. For a stand-alone dish, you could add fresh, chopped tomatoes and spoon the mixture on top of roasted aubergine. Add a bit of fresh chilli, top with yoghurt and you will have a wholesome and comforting vegetable main.

300g lentils

2–3 tbsp vegetable oil

3 onions, very roughly chopped

1 bay leaf

1 tsp dried thyme

3 carrots, cut into 2-cm chunks on the diagonal

4 stalks of celery with leaves, sliced

2 tbsp vegetable stock powder

Splash of olive oil

1 tsp Worcestershire sauce

Salt and white pepper

½ cup parsley, chopped

½ cup coriander, chopped

½ cup dill, chopped

Cook the lentils in plenty of boiling water until just tender, about 10 minutes. Drain and rinse briefly with cold water.

Sauté the onion in vegetable oil until translucent, about 9–12 minutes. Add the bay leaf and thyme and then the chopped carrots and celery. Continue to cook, stirring, until the vegetables are just beginning to soften (we want a bit of crunch but not raw), about 5 minutes. Add stock powder and ½ cup water. Cook for another 3–5 minutes. Remove from the stove and stir in the cooked lentils. Add a splash of olive oil, the Worcestershire sauce and check for seasoning with salt and white pepper. Finally, stir in all the herbs.

Serves 8

Slow-Roast Shoulder of Lamb

A slow-roasted lamb dish is always a coup. It is relatively trouble-free to prepare, flavourful and easy to serve. Although many cooks allow the lamb to spend 8 hours in the oven, I personally prefer a shorter cooking time. It is, of course, a matter of opinion, but I think that some flavour and texture might be sacrificed the longer the cooking time – 5 or 6 hours will also win you a meltingly tender piece of meat. A leg of lamb also works very well for slow-roasting in this way.

2 onions, peeled and quartered

3 large carrots, peeled and cut
    into large chunks

3 long sprigs rosemary

Small bunch thyme

8 cloves garlic, sliced in halves

2–2.5 kg shoulder or leg of lamb

2 splashes olive oil, for coating

Salt and white pepper

1–2 tsp curry powder or your
    favourite meat rub

1 cup white wine

1 cup strong chicken stock

Preheat the oven to 180°C.

In a heavy oven casserole or deep roasting dish, arrange the onions, carrots, herbs and 3 cloves of garlic.

Coat the lamb with a splash or two of olive oil. Squeeze the remaining garlic into every natural crevice as deep as you can into the meat or make your own small holes with a sharp knife so that you have garlic studding the leg or shoulder. Now season the meat well with salt and white pepper and, if using, rub with curry spices or flavour rub of your choosing. After all this intimacy, place the lamb on top of the onions, carrots and herbs and pour the wine and stock around the meat. Cover with a heavy lid or tightly wrap the dish in a double layer of foil. (If the meat is touching the foil, place a small sheet of baking paper between the meat and the foil to prevent any sticking.)

Place the dish in a 180°C oven and bake for 1 hour. After an hour, turn the heat down to 120°C for another 5 hours. Check the roasting dish after 4 hours to see how it's doing. Depending on how tender it is, you can decide whether you want to leave it in the oven for another 1–2 hours.

After all these hours in the oven, your lamb will have reduced in size but it will be very tender. Carefully remove the meat from the pot (you might need two hands beneath the meat to hold it together) and place it on a wooden board. Cover with foil while you gather the pan juices together in a pot. Lift the onions and carrots out with a slotted spoon. With a large spoon, scoop as much of the lamb fat off the pan juices as possible and cook the juices until they have reduced slightly.

To serve, place the lamb into a warmed serving dish, arrange the vegetables around the meat, and pull out whatever bones you can see. The meat will be so tender, that the bones are very easily removed. Serve immediately, spooning over the juices.

Serves 6–8 (accompanied by Vegetably Lentils)

* If you are making the Vegetably Lentils to accompany this dish, you could use the vegetables from this roast to stir through the lentils.

Ginger Fudge

These double ginger squares have a committed following at The Kitchen. Try them and you'll see why.

Base
1½ cup plain flour
1 tsp baking powder
1 tsp ground ginger
½ cup caster sugar
125g butter

Topping
150g butter
¼ cup Golden Syrup
2 cups icing sugar, sifted
1 tbsp ground ginger
½ cup roughly chopped
   crystallised ginger

Preheat oven to 180°C.

Line a 17 x 27-cm deep-sided baking tin with baking paper, covering the bottom and sides of the tin. Then place the flour, baking powder, ginger and caster sugar in the bowl of a food processor and pulse to sift. Add butter and process to resemble fine breadcrumbs – or rub in the butter by hand. Press the crumbs evenly over the base of the prepared tin. Bake for 25 minutes until golden brown.

To make the topping, place the butter and Golden Syrup in a saucepan and melt over a medium heat. Add icing sugar and ground ginger and cook for 1 minute, stirring constantly to combine until smooth. Stir in the crystallised ginger. Then pour the topping over the base and leave to cool and set. Once cooled, remove from the tin and cut into bars or squares. These Ginger Fudge bars will last for up to 5 days stored in an airtight container.

Makes 24+ squares

Prosperity Bars

These bars actually go by two names: one is a wish, "Prosperity Bar", the other a warning, "Brutality Bar".

Base
2 ¼ cups plain flour
¾ cups caster sugar
190g butter
1½ tsp baking powder

Caramel
2 tins condensed milk
125g salted peanuts
2 tsp butter

Chocolate
200g best dark chocolate

To make the caramel, put the two tins of condensed milk in a deep saucepan and cover generously with water. Cover with a lid and boil for 70 minutes. Do not let the pan run dry! Be sure that the tins are always covered with water. Remove from the saucepan and allow the tins of caramel to cool before opening.

Preheat the oven to 180°C. Line the base and sides of a 20 x 30 cm baking tin with baking paper. Place all the ingredients for the shortbread base into a food processor and process until the pastry comes together in a ball. Press the shortbread out into the base of the prepared tin and bake at 180°C for 20 minutes.

Empty 1½ tins of caramel into a deep saucepan. Add the 2 tsp butter and melt together over low heat. Stir in the peanuts.

While you are assembling the Prosperity Bars, set the chocolate to melt in a bowl set over boiling water.

Spread the caramel peanut mixture over the baked shortbread, and finally, spread the melted chocolate over the caramel. (A palette knife works best.) Leave to set in the fridge for 2 hours or more.

To cut into squares, lift the rectangle of Prosperity out of the tin and use a long sharp slicer or cook's knife, cutting down with a firm sharp stroke so as to not squish the filling.

Makes 24+ squares

other bits

Gomashio

I first ate this marvellous Japanese mixture at the Greyton home of my friend, Karen Thorn. We had it atop what I now call "Bananas in Pyjamas": rye toast, creamed cheese, sliced banana, honey and gomashio.

4 tsp sea salt

2 cups sesame seeds, unhulled (browner) or hulled (whiter)

Toast the salt in a dry pan for 1–2 minutes until it goes a little grey. Set aside. Then toast the sesame seeds in a dry pan until they are fragrant, popping here and there, and a light brown colour. Spread out to cool on a baking tray. Leave to cool.

In a coffee grinder or food processor, pulse the seeds and the salt together. You need a very rough mixture rather than a paste, so just do the briefest of pulses on your machine so that the seeds are just slightly ground and the salt distributed through the seeds.

Gomashio should keep up to 5 months stored in a glass jar with a lid, but should not be refrigerated. You will find all sorts of opportunities to use it!

* Some clever folk add other seeds, such as linseeds, or black sesame seeds and bits of seaweed. Sprinkled over brown rice, it is almost a complete food.

Sesame Dressing

Often, when people ask, "What is that … that flavour?", my answer is "It's sesame." This dressing is versatile – as delicious stirred through brown rice as it is on your favourite leaves.

¼ cup vegetable oil

1 tbsp sesame oil

1 tbsp rice vinegar

2 tbsp ponzu sauce or soya sauce

½–1 tsp chopped chilli (to taste)

White pepper (to taste)

1 tbsp runny honey (optional)

Whisk together in a bowl or shake in a jar.

Makes about ¾ cup

Harissa

This is a fierce North African chilli paste that is all heat and flavour. We use it in our Harissa Chickpeas and in our Chicken Medina.

1½ tsp caraway seeds
1½ tsp coriander seeds
100g red chillies, deseeded
4 cloves garlic
½ tsp salt
¼ cup sundried tomatoes, soaked
¼ cup olive oil

Dry toast the caraway and coriander seeds in a small pan until fragrant, about 3–4 minutes. Then place the fragrant seeds in a spice grinder and grind as fine as you can.
Place the chillies, garlic, salt and sundried tomato in a food processor and purée to a paste, slowly drizzling in the olive oil. Press into a jar and cover with oil to prevent oxidation. This Harissa should keep well in the fridge for a week. You can also freeze in small bags for later use.

Ching Ching

This is our signature magic seasoning or rub, which we use on our grilled chicken breasts and other meat and vegetable dishes.

1 tsp salt
1 tsp white pepper
2 tsp smoked paprika
1½ tsp sugar
½ tsp curry powder
   (or Cape Malay spice)
1 tbsp dried oregano
2 tsp sesame seeds (optional)

Combine all the ingredients, and voila!

Za'tar

Here is a taste of Turkey – although it might seem familiar to you wherever you may be. It's one of those flavours I describe as "biblical". It is great sprinkled on salads, mezze, yoghurt and even eggs.

2 tbsp dried oregano
2 tbsp dried thyme
3 tbsp sesame seeds
2 tsp ground sumac
1 tsp sea salt
2 tsp ground cumin

Combine all the ingredients.
Store in a jar in the fridge for up to a month.

Index

Thanks

For this book, we packed up crates of ingredients, along with batches of recipes, and sent them off to friends for testing in their own kitchens. I received fantastic feedback and an enormous amount of input from them all. I am especially thankful to Simon Travers and Gwen Maye, Nathalie Jehle, Elsabé Jehle, Sandy Ribbans and friends, Tracey Longstaff and friends, Elton Holland and his family, and sisters Barbara and Gail Jennings. What a wonderful service they have done us all!

The members of my team in my own kitchen are the real business behind the consistently delicious food we make at The Kitchen. It is craziness to produce the amount of food we do in our kitchen – cooking for the shop and for private parties at the same time! Only an efficient and dedicated team can pull it off with such aplomb. They are creative and resourceful and I am so proud to work with each one.

For Roxy and Russel and I, working together is pure joy. I get to pull out my collection of beautiful things and style my vision on a plate. This book is about the joy of creating something beautiful with Roxy's masterful art direction and design and Russel's seamless photographic magic. Without a doubt, ours is friendship of a lifetime!

My thanks also go to Bridget Impey and our publishers Jacana Media who have again trusted us to make something good. We love working with you! And my very clever artist and wordsmith friend, Peter van Straten (www.petervanstraten.co.za), read my manuscript and Sean Fraser polished it.

To all who visit and frequent The Kitchen, thank you for your friendship and encouragement.

My children, Ben and Maggie, create the happy, thankful place in which this book is written. And my husband, David, has been beside me, my partner and my sanctuary. Thank you, my Sweetheart.

Karen

Photography: Russel Wasserfall

Art Direction & Design: Roxanne Spears

Styling: Karen Dudley & Roxanne Spears

Typesetting: Ross Campbell

Proof Reader: Sean Fraser

Image Processing: Sarah Kate Schäfer

Holiday Pics (page 93): David Mallinson

For Jacana:

Publishing Director: Bridget Impey

Production Manager: Kerrie Barlow

First published in 2013 by Jacana Media (Pty) Ltd
10 Orange Street, Sunnyside,
Auckland Park, 2092, South Africa
+27 11 628 3200, www.jacana.co.za

Text © 2013 Karen Dudley
Photography © 2013 Russel Wasserfall
Design © 2013 Roxanne Spears
All rights reserved. No part of this book may be reproduced in any form and by any means, electronic or mechanical, including photocopying, without permission in writing from the authors

ISBN 978-1-4314-0841-2

Printed by Craft Print, Singapore
Job No. 002067

See a complete list of Jacana titles at www.jacana.co.za